Pain

...ok is to be returned on or before
...e last date stamped below.

Health Psychology

Series editors:
Sheila Payne and Sandra Horn

Published titles

Psychology and Health Promotion
Paul Bennett and Simon Murphy

Pain: theory, research and intervention
Sandra Horn and Marcus Munafò

Pain
Theory, research and
intervention

Sandra Horn and
Marcus Munafò

Open University Press
Buckingham • Philadelphia

Open University Press
Celtic Court
22 Ballmoor
Buckingham
MK18 1XW

and

1900 Frost Road, Suite 101
Bristol, PA 19007, USA

First published 1997

9 707083

W L 704

A catalogue record of this book is available from the British Library

ISBN   0 335 19688 8 (pbk)   0 335 19689 6 (hbk)

Library of Congress Cataloging-in-Publication Data
Horn, Sandra.
    Pain: theory, research, and intervention / Sandra Horn and Marcus Munafò.
        p.   cm. — (Health psychology)
    Includes bibliographical references and index.
    ISBN 0–335–19689–6 (hb). — ISBN 0–335–19688–8 (pb)
    1. Pain.   2. Pain—Psychological aspects.   3. Clinical health psychology.   I. Munafò, Marcus, 1972–   .   II. Title.   III. Series.
    [DNLM: 1. Pain.   WL 704 H813p 1997]
    RB127.H68   1997
    616'.0472—dc21
    DNLM/DLC
    for Library of Congress   96–29576
                                                                          CIP

Typeset by Graphicraft Typesetters Ltd, Hong Kong
Printed in Great Britain by St Edmundsbury Press Ltd,
Bury St Edmunds, Suffolk

Contents

Series editors' foreword

This new series of books in health psychology is designed to support post-graduate and postqualification studies in psychology, nursing, medicine and paramedical sciences, as well as the establishment of health psychology within the undergraduate psychology curriculum. Health psychology is growing rapidly as a field of study. Concerned as it is with the application of psychological theories and models in the promotion and maintenance of health, and the individual and interpersonal aspects of adaptive behaviour in illness and disability, health psychology has a wide remit and a potentially important role to play in the future.

In this book, theory, research and interventions in the universal phenomenon of pain, an issue of central concern in health psychology, are explored. Melzack and Wall's theory of a gating mechanism in pain perception represented a conceptual leap forward, and was the beginning of an inter-disciplinary approach in which the interwoven nature of psychological, neurological and physiological factors in pain were acknowledged and developed. The first part of the book is concerned with the history of thought about pain and the development of theories and research. In the second part, the practical applications of knowledge and theory are examined. Psychology has made a number of crucially important contributions to this field of study, and it is timely to review the current status of theory, research and practice in pain, to set them in the context of historical development, and to look to possibilities for the future.

Sheila Payne and Sandra Horn

 # Preface

This book is designed to introduce students to the theory, research and clinical application of psychological and behavioural models in pain.

Psychology has made and continues to make a huge contribution to the understanding of pain phenomena, mechanisms and treatments. Pain provides a rich field of study in which conceptual challenges are constantly thrown up, and traditional disciplinary boundaries are breached. It is a significant factor in many people's lives, as a relatively transient phenomenon which is the most frequently presented symptom in medical interviews. At the other end of its scale of influence, it can exist as an intrusive, long-lasting and pervasive source of disability. In many circumstances, indeed most, pain serves a valuable function as an alarm signal for actual or impending tissue damage and injury, allowing the individual to behave in an appropriate way, signalling for help, avoiding the noxious stimulus, and so on. One point which will be highlighted throughout this volume, however, is the potential that these adaptive behaviours have to become maladaptive over time, contributing to the disability of patients with pain that does not resolve. The processes by which this happens are not yet fully understood.

This book is constructed in two complementary halves: theoretical issues are considered in Chapter 1, beginning with the historical evolution of pain theories, from simple neurological models and on to the conceptual leap presented by Melzack and Wall in the gate control theory of pain. This is complemented in Chapter 2 by an exploration of pain mechanisms, focusing on the role of physiological features of pain mechanisms which represent possible correlates of psychological influences on pain response, such as endogenous opioids and plastic features of the central nervous system. The findings of laboratory studies, and their relationship to ecological situations, are considered in Chapter 3, along with limitations of this approach. Chapter 4 presents a conclusion to the debate concerning the degree to which physiological and psychological models are compatible by giving an account of the relationship between acute pain and chronic pain, and the differential role of physiological and psychological factors across these.

The second half of the book is concerned with individual differences in pain response and pain behaviour, in particular personal, social and cultural differences (Chapter 5), which in turn raises issues of measurement and treatment, discussed in Chapters 6 and 7. Special consideration is given to issues such as the assessment of pain in children and the factors of importance in, for example, cancer pain. This critical exegesis presents ways in which the theoretical findings discussed in the first chapters can be integrated with practice in an attempt to improve the treatment and management of pain.

Theories of pain

I can sympathize with people's pains, but not with their
pleasures. There is something curiously boring about
somebody else's happiness.

(Huxley 1946)

Summary

The historical development of pain research and understanding of pain
phenomena are discussed, with reference to both philosophical and scientific thought, and the degree to which changes in both of these have pro-
gressed largely in parallel. Early scientific theories of pain are described and
their inadequacies highlighted, in particular the pain phenomena which
these early models were unable to explain. This provides the basis for
the introduction of the dominant conceptual model of pain now broadly
accepted, with an emphasis on presenting this as an important conceptual
shift which has led to a renaissance of interest in the field, rather than a
model built on entirely new findings. Finally, some of the issues to be
discussed in later chapters are briefly introduced, in the context of the
dominant theme of different levels of explanation being appropriate as a
function of the specific question asked, so that a psychological explanation
may be used in one context and a physiological explanation in another. The
crucial point is the extent to which such alternative explanations reflect
different aspects of the same underlying phenomena.

Introduction

Pain is an unusual phenomenon, and this is reflected in pain research. While
pain experience is undeniably a very personal and individual thing, the
majority of research and thought in this area has, for the past three hundred
years, emphasized the mechanistic nature of pain. Although this can be
traced to the behaviourist description of pain responses by Descartes (1664),
the foundations lie further back in the history of thought. Sextus reports
the Epicurean claim that 'it is impossible for what is productive . . . of pain

not to be painful' (Everson 1991), which implies linear causality, with no modulating factors acting between the stimulus and the response. This was subsequently developed by those such as Descartes, who argued that pain is evidenced by the withdrawal of the relevant body part from the noxious stimulus as a result of nerve action – the pain mechanism, and consequent behaviour, is distinct and separate from the individual's experience of pain, and can be described in a simple mechanistic, behaviourist way. More recently, linguistic philosophers following the example of Wittgenstein have contended that pain is defined by public pain behaviour, so that it is meaningless to talk of pain as a private experience of which, in others, we can have only inferred knowledge. If a person is crying out in distress, and the context is appropriate, what other criteria could we adduce for concluding that the person was in pain? We can, and do, say quite justifiably that we can *know* someone to be in pain, although there is certainly scope for deception. This is central to the confusion, where pain is both regarded as private and yet measurable and knowable, and is largely the result of an imperfect understanding of the subtleties of pain as a phenomenon (see Grounds 1987).

This philosophical development, certainly the mechanistic behaviourism exemplified by Descartes, has had a pervasive influence on scientific investigation into pain phenomena and mechanisms. Indeed, in many ways the development of philosophical thought has paralleled the development of scientific thought, with the move away from emphasizing the importance of any private experience (indeed questioning the very meaningfulness of this privacy) coming at a similar time to the work of Fordyce (Fordyce *et al.* 1968), with attendant emphasis on public expression of pain. The logical behaviourism of more recent philosophy (Jacquette 1985) emphasizes that external factors are the important criteria in understanding mental experiences, including pain, and any discussion of internal mental objects ('pain events', for example) is meaningless and irrelevant (Graham 1993). Until the mid-1960s the history of research into the anatomy and physiology of pain was typified by attempts to isolate specific pain transmission fibres and receptors which formed a unique and complete system. Specificity theories of pain (see pp. 3–5) could be interpreted as Cartesian theory translated into modern scientific parlance, and in keeping with the dualism of Descartes, psychological factors tended to be ignored or dismissed as distinct from the 'real' pain. It is only recently that attempts have been made, most notably by Ronald Melzack and Patrick Wall, to break this philosophical hegemony.

Specificity theories of pain proposed that the activation of specific pain receptors and transmitters, as a result of injury, projected to an isolated pain centre, via a spinal pain pathway. Causation was linear, and psychological factors were ignored, to the extent that injury was directly equated with pain, as proposed by Epicurus (342–270 BC). The result of this was that pain cases which could not be accommodated by this model were regarded as in some sense not 'real'; this had the consequence that phantom limb pain patients or chronic pain patients with no demonstrable or discernible organic pathology, for example, were commonly referred to psychiatrists. It is worth making clear at the outset that simply because no physical pathology can be detected it does not follow that it does not exist; this point will be of more relevance in future sections, in particular with reference to chronic pain.

This approach, where anomalies which cannot be accounted for by existing models are ignored, is simply bad science, and a growing number of reported pain case anomalies led to an impetus for more comprehensive models of pain. The most important of these attempts was patterning (or pattern) theory, which in fact refers to a number of various, closely related theories (see pp. 5–6). Central summation of pain fibre activity in the dorsal horns or a balance of activity between large-diameter and small-diameter pain fibres were two suggestions intended to account for various pain anomalies (Melzack 1993). While these theories were generally vague, they had the advantage of acknowledging that a simple, linear model of pain causation is inadequate. Where these models failed was in their continued resistance to accepting a more active role for the brain (as opposed to a passive, receptive role) and, specifically, psychological processes.

This failure to acknowledge adequately the role of brain processes was finally addressed in 1965 by Melzack and Wall in their paper 'Pain mechanisms: a new theory'. The central feature of this theory is that pain fibre transmission is modulated at the base of the spinal column by a 'gate'. The extent to which this gate is open or closed determines the degree to which pain fibre transmissions pass to the brain stem and cerebral cortex, and consequently the degree to which pain is felt. This gate may be opened or closed by either ascending signals (such as the balance of activation between large-diameter and small-diameter pain fibres) or descending signals (brain processes related to, for example, level of anxiety). Thus, athletes who continue playing without noticing they have injured themselves are unaware of the damage because the signals ascending from the site of injury are blocked at the gate by other descending factors, such as intense concentration, as well as, possibly, further ascending sensory signals. Where specificity and patterning theories struggle, gate control theory appears to offer a possible explanation for phenomena such as these. This chapter will explore the development of specificity and patterning theories, and their inadequacies, which has led to the ascendance of gate control theory.

Specificity theory

The simplicity of theories which attempt to identify unique channels along which pain signals are transmitted and inevitably result in the sensation of pain is perhaps best summarized by Descartes. His proposal was that the causation from injury to pain acts in the same way as a bell-ringing mechanism, so that 'by pulling at one end of a rope one makes to strike at the same instant a bell which hangs at the other end' (Melzack and Wall 1982: 150). This was the conception which would remain dominant, indeed supreme, in western medicine until the mid-1960s, with only minor development to facilitate the incorporation of these ideas into modern medical parlance.

Modern specificity theories reached the peak of their development between the middle of the nineteenth century and the beginning of the twentieth century. This was begun by Muller's strong contention that the brain received information about external stimuli only via the sensory nerves (Muller 1842). Given that pain fell into this category of stimulation, information about painful stimuli could be carried only by sensory nerves. The strength of this paradigm shift in understanding was such that DuBois-Reymond (in Boring 1942) suggested that if the auditory nerve were to be connected to the visual cortex we would see thunder (Melzack and Wall 1982).

While the work of Muller advanced the Cartesian conception of pain transmission into modern medicine and physiology, it was von Frey (1894) who was to develop a more complete specificity theory of pain. From his assumption that the human skin comprises a multitude of unique sensory 'spots' for either touch, cold, warmth or pain, von Frey moved on to suggest that free-nerve endings were specific pain receptors. This was based on two facts: that pain 'spots' are found almost everywhere on the skin, and that free-nerve endings are by far the most commonly found. According to von Frey, then, the specific pain receptors had been discovered, with others moving on to seek specific pathways from the receptors to the spinal cord and then the brain. This search again relied on the Cartesian notion that there existed a direct link between a peripheral receptor and a specific brain site.

Extensions to von Frey's theory included the ascription of unique types of pain (sharp versus dull, for example) to different pain fibre types, so that theorists began to speak of A-delta fibre pain and C-fibre pain – as opposed to simply A-delta fibre *transmission*. The spinothalamic tract was also identified as crucial for the transmission of pain information, and has since become referred to as the 'pain pathway' (Melzack and Wall 1982). Debate concerning the exact location, in the brain stem and thalamus, of the nuclei which receive pain information continues.

The valuable legacy of specificity theories and attendant research has been the description of the extent of specificity in peripheral sensory fibres, although specificity theories were characterized by an attempt to ascribe too great a degree of specificity to the peripheral sensory nervous system. The weakness of specificity theory, as described by von Frey and, with only minor modifications, others is *not* the assumption that each sensation corresponds to a unique receptor type, although this is clearly incorrect and extends the degree of peripheral specificity too far. More damaging is the assumption that there exists a direct and invariant relationship between a physical stimulus and a sensation felt by the individual. The term 'pain receptor' implies that stimulation of this receptor will invariably result in the sensation of pain, and only result in the sensation of pain, which returns us to the understanding of pain elucidated by Epicurus (see p. 1). This is obviously insufficient, and a single example will serve to illustrate this: American service personnel severely wounded in action reported very little pain, in some cases none at all, even though comparable injury on a civilian ward would require extensive pain medication (Beecher 1959). There has been debate regarding the mechanism subsuming this effect, with an argument being that such analgesia is found to some degree in all subjects with major physical trauma, possibly as the result of endogenous opioid release. Melzack and his colleagues have demonstrated that 37 per cent of civilians with severe physical trauma do not feel pain at the time of injury, with this persisting for up to nine hours after the injury (Larbig 1991). What is more likely, however, is that the explanation offered by Beecher, that the meaning of the injury mediates the pain response, is also a factor. This is supported by a comparison of Beecher's results with those of Melzack: 66 per cent of Beecher's soldiers did not experience pain as a result of their injuries (Larbig 1991). Similar tissue damage does not necessarily result in similar pain across individuals, and this is in part due to a constellation of psychological, social and cultural variables. It was the assumption of psychological specificity which was most damaging to specificity theories and led to the development of alternative, patterning theories of pain.

Patterning theory

A reaction against the specificity theory first proposed by von Frey in fact began before its inadequacies had been fully described. Evidence from late-stage syphilis patients, who sometimes report unusual pain as a response to mild stimuli, such as burning pain when repeatedly touched by a warm stimulus, suggested to Goldscheider that some form of central summation process was required if pain mechanisms were to be fully understood (Goldscheider 1884). The important feature of this new theory was that transmission of peripheral sensory information was summated at the dorsal horn, with pain information being transmitted only if the level of ouput at the dorsal horn exceeded a threshold. Theories of this type, which mostly attempt to account for pathological pain states, recognize the importance of the balance of input activity and have stemmed from the seminal work of Goldscheider.

The most simple, and vague, variant of patterning theory suggests that the sensation of pain is the result of spatial and temporal patterns of neural transmission, as opposed to individual transmission pathways unique to pain information. The theory fails in its insistence that all free nerve endings are alike and non-specific, so that they may receive any sensory information. This is contrary to physiological evidence, which suggests a great deal of receptor specificity.

Various pathological pain states have already been identified as a motivating factor in the search for alternatives to specificity theories. Phantom limb pain, for example, is difficult to explain using a pain specificity model, and Livingston (1943) was the first to suggest a model to account for the summation phenomena in this syndrome. This central summation theory relied on the postulation of closed circuits in the spinal cord which, when triggered by usually non-noxious stimuli, lead to pain information being transmitted to the brain. In the case of phantom limb pain, the initial trauma leads to abnormal stimulation in these circuits. This, in turn, can lead to further stimulation at the damaged limb which creates a positive feedback loop and a maintenance of the abnormal state. Once this state has become self-sustaining it becomes difficult to interrupt it – surgical removal of the input sources may not be sufficient. However, one theoretical consequence of this theory and others like it is that lesions at the spinal cord should abolish the pain. While this is true in some cases of phantom limb pain, this does not happen consistently.

An extension of summation theories is the theory that summation is prevented in normal subjects by a dedicated input-modulating system. Pain information fibres are supposed to be inhibited by transmission along larger-diameter fibres, with transmission to the central nervous system (CNS) being the result of the balance of activity between these groups of fibres. A relative increase in the number of small-diameter fibres compared to large-diameter fibres would result in increased pain information transmission, greater summation and, as a result, greater pain. This theory goes some way to explaining the failure of spinal cord lesions in abolishing pathological pain states in all cases, and is markedly more comprehensive in the pain phenomena it can explain than simple specificity theories. Most encouragingly, this theory is consistent with the physiological observation that there is a relative loss of large fibres following peripheral nerve damage. Theories such as these, developed primarily in the late 1950s, represent a major advance in the conceptual understanding of pain mechanisms, and may be regarded as the paradigm shift which prefaced the advance of the gate control theory of pain.

Pain phenomena

The move away from a Cartesian understanding of pain phenomena was largely the result of pain cases which clearly could not be explained by a simple model, and patterning theories represent the first stage of this move.

Phantom limb pain has already been identified as one pathological pain state where the pain cannot be related to any obvious physical injury or pathology. There are, however, many other similar phenomena.

Cases of congenital universal insensitivity to pain (CUIP) are rare, but provide a valuable test area for pain research. Reports of CUIP date back to at least 1891 (McMurray 1975) and are typified by an early detection of general insensitivity to painful stimuli, with no attendant generalized sensory loss. Subjects with CUIP usually die young, as any pathology which is primarily identified by painful symptoms, such as appendicitis, goes undetected. One apparently simple explanation of this phenomenon would be that the specific pain transmission pathway was in some way incomplete, so that pain information could not reach the pain centre in the brain. Unfortunately the physiological evidence from CUIP patients post-mortem appears to contradict this possibility: 'We have failed, therefore, to demonstrate any anatomical abnormalities of those nervous system structures thought to be concerned with the transmission, elaboration and perception of pain impulses' (McMurray 1975). Cases of CUIP, therefore, present another difficulty for specificity theories, not least because the surgical removal of complete pain transmission systems in animal subjects does not result in a condition similar to CUIP. Patterning theories fail for quite opposite reasons: these theories dismiss the great deal of physiological specificity which does exist in somesthetic systems and instead place the work of explanation on patterns of firing which cannot be observed. This makes patterning theories not only difficult to disprove but also of limited explanatory value.

Something apparently opposite in nature to CUIP is Lesch-Niehan disease (Melzack and Wall 1982), which is characterized by self-mutilation and retarded development, both physical and mental. The self-mutilation is preceded by a sudden exhibition of pain behaviour, so that the subject apparently is in intolerable pain and initiates self-mutilation in response to this. As in the case of CUIP, there are no apparent physiological abnormalities post-mortem. So here we have evidence that pain without injury, as well as injury without pain, can occur in subjects with apparently normal pain transmission systems.

Once again, this pathological state may be, at least phenomenologically, related to less extreme and more common cases. Loeser (1980) reports that 70 per cent of chronic low back pain patients (the most common form of chronic pain) have no discernible physical pathology. Phantom limb pain also falls into this category of pain after apparent healing of the initial injury. A condition which shares many of the characteristics of phantom limb pain is causalgia, which is typified by a very intense, burning pain. Here the original cause appears to be some physical injury which, when healed, leaves the patient pathologically sensitive to neutral stimuli, which can initiate a painful episode. Central nervous system changes have been suggested as the primary factor in causalgia, but the aetiology and mechanism remains unclear. Finally, a class of pain syndromes similar in their properties to both phantom limb pain and causalgia are the neuralgias. Rather than physical trauma being the initial cause of the syndrome (as in causalgia), the neuralgias may be brought about by peripheral nerve damage resulting from viral infection, diabetes, poor circulation, vitamin deficiency, or poison ingestion. Essentially, any condition which results in damage to peripheral nerve fibres may be the cause of neuralgic pain (Melzack and Wall 1982). In all of these cases apparent tissue healing may mask the continuance of neural tissue scarring and neuromata, in turn leading to abnormal peripheral activity.

While cases of CUIP, Lesch-Niehan disease, causalgia, the neuralgias and so on are spectacular and go far in providing support for the position that specificity and patterning theories of pain are insufficient, it is dangerous to draw conclusions solely from pathological cases. However, somewhat similar phenomena occur in normal subjects. It is common for injured subjects to report that they feel no pain until some time after the injury occurred – occasionally several hours (Melzack and Wall 1982). This has been typified by the work of Beecher (1959) reporting widespread lack of pain in very severely injured soldiers, so that tissue damage did not appear to be a sufficient condition for pain, as detailed above. It is clear that insensitivity to pain has both pathological and normal manifestations and (as briefly discussed above) this is likely to be describable with reference to both psychological and physiological models.

In the 1950s, Zborowski (1952) pioneered research into cultural differences in response to painful stimuli, and these findings are now well established, with differences in expression of pain symptoms, anxiety levels and response to treatment varying across cultures. These differences not only are in pain tolerance and pain threshold (see Chapter 3 on laboratory studies), but also appear to be reflected in the semantics of linguistic pain expression. Indeed, one problem of cross-cultural pain research lies in the translation of English pain descriptors into other languages, thereby introducing a distorting factor. Nevertheless, it is still rare for clinicians to incorporate an understanding of this cultural and linguistic variation in their diagnosis and treatment: acceptance of the role of psychological and social factors in modulating pain response is still limited by a tacit acceptance of the Cartesian model of pain information transmission by many clinicians. This cultural variation in response to painful stimuli is related to individual differences in response which are also found. The concept of a pain-prone personality has been suggested by, among others, Sternbach (1978), and strongly implies that there must be an active role for psychological characteristics in any adequate model of pain mechanisms. The pain-prone person is characteristically anxious and depressed (Shanfield and Killingworth 1977), and these factors have in themselves been found to reduce pain tolerance, for example, and influence vulnerability to post-operative pain. While psychiatric and psychophysiological explanations of the pain-prone personality differ, this may simply reflect different explanatory requirements in these two fields, and consequently different levels of explanation.

Furthermore, it is possible to develop techniques by which pain toler-ance levels may be elevated, with one celebrated case being that of T.E. Lawrence, who, when asked how he could extinguish the flame of a candle very slowly, said that the trick was 'not to mind the pain'. If pain trans-mission systems are simple and mechanistic, phenomena like these simply should not occur. More empirical examples of the same phenomena exist, with athletes being able to tolerate higher levels of pain, apparently through the use of elaborate strategies designed to distract oneself from the pain. This is further reflected in the development of cognitive interventions which allow acute and chronic pain patients to endure and even modify their pain (Eccleston 1995), and the use of professional psychologists in sport to allow athletes to reach higher levels of performance by employing similar strat-egies. Regarding the latter, at least one British gold medal at the Barcelona Olympics in 1992 was credited in part by the medal-winner to such strat-egies. It is interesting that individuals with such a requirement tend to develop such strategies spontaneously, but these can be enhanced by the intervention of a sports psychologist, and that furthermore there appears to be great scope for individual differences in this capacity.

It was this increasing body of evidence, that specificity theories of pain did not account for the variety of pain phenomena which were reliably and repeatedly reported, both in pathological and normal populations, which led to the development of patterning theories in an attempt to account fully for the observed data. This growing tension in the existing paradigm, however, culminated in the development of the gate control theory of pain (Melzack and Wall 1965) and the adoption of a more complete conception of what any model of pain mechanisms must entail.

Gate control theory

Melzack and Wall in *The Challenge of Pain* (1982) summarize evidence such as that presented above by stating that any comprehensive theory of pain must be able to account for the following:

◆ the high degree of physiological specialization of receptor-fibre units and of pathways in the central nervous system
◆ the role of temporal and spatial patterning in the transmission of informa-tion in the nervous system
◆ the clinical phenomena of spatial and temporal summation, spread of pain and persistence of pain after healing
◆ the influence of psychological processes on pain perception and response.

As outlined previously, the vital and most novel feature of the gate control theory of Melzack and Wall is the gate itself, a neural mechanism supposed to exist in the dorsal horns of the spinal cord, which modulates the passage of pain information signals from the periphery to the central nervous system. The degree to which the gate is open or closed depends on ascending signals from the peripheral nerves and descending signals from the central nervous system. Ascending signals consist of a balance between the level of activity in large-diameter (A-beta) fibres and small-diameter (A-delta and C) fibres. Clearly this borrows a substantial amount of the patterning theory literature, assimilating it into a more comprehensive model which presents the opportunity for empirical testing. The nature of descending signals, while being the most visionary element of the model, was unclear at the time of the theory's formulation, but was intended to account for the role of psychological factors, such as anxiety, on pain response.

It is important to realize that pain information signals must be modulated at the gate, and allowed to pass, before the individual is in pain. In other words, the correlate of pain experience and behaviour is one or a set of central processes, and these central processes are related to injury and peripheral nerve activity only in a derivative way. While it is misleading to speak of pain as being identical with specific central activity, it is certainly more closely related to this than anything else. To explain this further, while tissue damage defines our understanding of pain, given that tissue damage is neither a necessary nor a sufficient condition for pain, we must look elsewhere for the physiological correlate of pain. This has been expounded more clearly in the philosophical literature than in the psychological, but there is an increasing awareness of the literature across both fields. The crucial work in determining whether or not an individual is in pain, however, is done at the site of the gate, and for this reason the entire central nervous system must be taken into account when pain mechanisms are considered.

A large part of the value of this new conception of pain mechanisms is the ability it has to account for both injury occurring without pain being felt and pain being felt without any apparent injury. If we move away from viewing tissue damage as being the prime determinant of whether an individual is in pain, and instead regard CNS activity, particularly whether or not the gate is open, as being this determinant, these apparent anomalies can be accounted for with ease, at least at a conceptual level. The specific mechanisms which subsume this general concept will be discussed in more detail in Chapter 2. So, in the case of injury without pain, we can contend that pain information signals are blocked at the gate, either because of other peripheral nerve activity which is inhibitory, or because of descending signals from the higher CNS, the exact nature of which remains unclear. As far as pain without apparent injury is concerned any explanation must rely to a greater extent on descending CNS signals, and (as will be shown in Chapter 2) there has been an abundance of recent research which identifies possible mechanisms for this. As will be seen, much of this research has been motivated by the great number of cases of chronic pain without identifiable physical pathology which exist, rather than the rarer patho-logical pain states.

There is substantial evidence that the gate operates at the site of the substantia gelatinosa, which receives signals from both large- and small-diameter fibres and also influences the activity of cells which project to the higher CNS. Peripheral nerve activity, carrying information about tem-perature, pressure and chemical changes, is supposed to excite spinal cord T cells, determined by the temporal and spatial patterns of this activity. These T cells then project to the higher CNS, via the gate, which modu-lates the extent to which this information passes unhindered. This modu-lation at the gate may be achieved in one or both of two broad mechanisms: nerve impulses may be blocked, either at nerve terminals or by decreasing transmitter substance release; alternatively, the excitability of cells to arriv-ing impulses may be decreased. The specifics of these alternative mechanisms is beyond the scope of this book, but it is important to realize that both mechanisms act, probably synergistically. It is the A-delta and C-fibre activ-ity which directly acts on T cells, as modulated by the mechanisms described above. The pattern of activity in these fibres determines important phe-nomena such as summation of activity, prolonged activity, and the spread of activity to other body areas. As this model becomes able to account for a broader range of pain phenomena, so must we increasingly regard pain mechanisms as in fact an interacting, synergistic range of mechanisms which serve functions other than simply pain information transmission.

A large part of the synergistic nature of this model comes from the role of descending influences on the gate. There is an abundance of psycho-logical evidence that factors such as attention, anxiety, past experience and personality, among others, can modulate the relationship between physical pathology and pain, some of which will be explored in more detail later. These are not functions which are specific to pain information transmis-sion, but have a great effect on it, and a similar case may be made for the broader role of the physiological elements of the model. Certainly at the time the gate control theory was first formulated, and even on subsequent revision in the 1980s, the mechanisms which subsume these effects remained unclear. Nevertheless, the theory made allowance for these factors to be incorporated, and recently advances have been made, both in delineating which higher CNS, cognitive and emotional functions modulate pain experi-ence and in outlining the mechanisms by which these act. Broadly speaking, the concept of a gating mechanism is now accepted; as Wall states: 'That a gate control exists is no longer open to doubt but its functional role and its detailed mechanism remain open for speculation and for experiment' (quoted in Larbig 1991). Although, the specifics of the modulation of pain information transmission remain open to debate, the concept of a gate is no longer controversial. Some aspects of the theory are controversial, most notably the extent to which the gate can be 'opened', thereby sensitizing the individual to painful stimulation, but the shift in understanding is complete.

The great strength of the gate control theory is its ability to integrate psychological, behavioural and physiological elements and present them as different levels of explanation (see Grahek 1991) of a single holistic system (Schneider and Karoly 1983; Ciccone and Grzesiak 1984). Indeed, its value is not in its description of the mechanisms of pain response but in the conceptual shift which its acceptance requires. That is, pain information transmission is not subsumed by a simple, linear system, but a synergistic pattern of interactions across physiological and psychological systems, with only limited specificity to noxious stimulation. The challenge is to develop this conceptual shift to incorporate the gamut of pain phenomena and factors which influence pain response. This variety in individual response to a given stimulus is what presents the greatest attraction in pain research.

Developmental issues exist, both theoretical and clinical, with debate concerning the extent to which pain responses in children are comparable to those in adults (Craig *et al.* 1993; Stevens and Johnston 1993). This extends to a question of how we may adequately assess pain in children, given these potential differences in pain information transmission and further differences in expression and interpretation. Children display a range of responses to pain, both adaptive and maladaptive (Siegel and Smith 1989), but these do not necessarily mirror the response found in adults. Again as in adults, assessment may be by either self-report or behavioural recording, but children present unique problems (Lavigne *et al.* 1986), and these are frequently compounded by the common assumption that similar assessment tools to those used with adults can be used with children. At the other end of the developmental spectrum, older individuals tend to suffer more pain, in particular chronic pain (Gibson *et al.* 1994), as a result of increased susceptibility to disease and illness, and as such have altered responses to pain, psychologically, behaviourally and, possibly, physiologically. For example, it has been suggested that pain complaint is reduced in elderly people (Gibson *et al.* 1994), so that assessors have to be aware of such differences if they are to fulfil their role adequately. Sex differences have also been the focus of much research, with the relationship between sex and pain appearing to be both subtle and complex. Explanations include those adopting a social learning model, so that women are more likely to label a given sensation as painful, and those physiological models that rely on, for example, hormonal fluctuations (Niven and Carroll 1993). This individual variation in response to painful stimulation extends to cultural differences, and while the nature of these differences is well established at a descriptive level, the explanation remains largely unresolved. Largely experimental studies have shown, for example, lower pain tolerance levels in Italian subjects when compared to English subjects (cf. Zatzick and Dimsdale 1990), while others have shown differences in the treatment offered to patients on the (presumably implicit) basis of their race (Villaruel 1995). Some have attempted to relate psychosocial and cultural explanations for these differences, usually relying on some variant of social learning theory, to gate control theory (Bates 1987), which emphasizes the interdependence of these models. As a counterpoint, evidence for the consistency of pain responses is also revealing: facial expressions of pain appear to be consistent across modalities of pain induction (Prkachin 1992), and it seems likely that, while sensitivity to pain varies across individuals and cultures, pain behaviours are broadly universal. Finally, the notion of a pain-prone personality (described briefly on p. 8 and in more detail in subsequent chapters) is related to differences in pain response in psychiatric patients. These include a relationship between pain and anxiety (Jensen 1988) in non-psychotic patients, which extends to the description of pain as a symptom of emotional disturbance. This relationship between the physical and affective dimensions of pain is perhaps the most pervasive in the literature (Kremer *et al.* 1983).

These phenomena have presumably always existed; however, a conceptual shift in the role of pain responses in the broader context of normal (and sometimes abnormal) human behaviour, such as that offered by gate control theory, allows for these phenomena to be incorporated into an explanation which has both psychological and physiological components (Craig 1984). This broader understanding of the theoretical issues present in pain research has been accompanied by a relative open-mindedness to methods of pain control which until recently were regarded as somewhat fringe ideas. An example of this is acupuncture, which is now widely accepted as a valid and beneficial method of pain control and has attracted rigorous research into the mechanics of this (cf. Price *et al.* 1984; Yang *et al.* 1984). While explanatory models which were alien to western medicine played a role in the exclusion of acupuncture among western clinicians, it is now apparent that existing models (i.e. gate control) are able to accommodate acupuncture phenomena without modification (Lewith and Kenyon 1984), although this is still the subject of some debate.

This points perhaps to a weakness in the gate control theory: that it is still largely a physiological model, with reference made to psychological factors but little scope for testable hypotheses to be developed on the basis of this. Indeed, Melzack and Wall themselves have contributed little to the non-physiological elaboration of the model, preferring instead to focus on the specifics of the physiological aspects. As an alternative, some have proposed the use of signal detection theory as a means of developing testable hypotheses regarding the distinction between sensory and response bias changes in pain report and behaviour (Rollman 1992). This is a psychophysical model which can be applied to much of the research outlined in the next section, and attempts to outline the detection processes required to distinguish between signal and noise (e.g. painful stimulation and distraction) (Malow and Dougher 1979). The value of this approach is that it allows specific predictions to be made in specific directions (crudely, for example, focusing on another task produces noise which masks the signal produced by painful stimulation). This approach, of course, is by no means irreconcilable with gate control theory – indeed, the two may be most useful if regarded as alternative models of the same underlying conception. While gate control theory represents a major theoretical and conceptual advance, it should not be thought of as an absolute descriptive model; instead it is best to regard it as a convenient shorthand to allow a clearer understanding of the interactive role of a variety of factors. The pattern of the activity in the peripheral nervous system determines the activity which projects to the central nervous system, and is in turn determined by descending activity from the CNS. Signal detection theory turns on a similar assumption but instead emphasizes the role of the CNS, in particular the brain, as opposed to the peripheral nervous system and the spinal cord.

It is this strength of integration which will be emphasized and drawn on in subsequent chapters. Physiological elements of pain mechanisms which have specific relevance to psychological and behavioural factors in pain sensation will be described in some detail and related to these psychological and behavioural factors. This is not a physiology text, however, and it is the psychosocial and behavioural influences on pain which will be investigated in detail. There will follow a discussion of laboratory studies of pain and their relevance to both theory and clinical practice. Both acute and chronic dimensions of pain will be described, as well as the limitations of this simple, dichotic understanding, with an emphasis being placed on the clinical importance of theoretical findings. This attempt to integrate both theory and clinical practice, domains which in the past have often remained separate, is an extension of attempts to understand pain in the broader context of interacting systems acting at different levels of explanation, so that answers should be regarded as appropriate to the question, rather than correct or incorrect in an absolute sense.

Conclusion

The relationship between pain and injury presents us with a number of apparent anomalies, which early models of pain transmission were unable to resolve adequately. Both specificity and patterning theories are poor explanatory models and offered little in the way of testable hypotheses. Gate control theory unified elements of both of these models (or groups of models), as well as adding a number of other elements including a role for descending influences, thereby introducing the potential for psychological, social and behavioural factors (such as past experience and affective state) to be explained by the same model as explained peripheral sensory nerve activity. This integration of physiological and psychological models represented a conceptual leap which was necessary if our understanding of pain were to develop. The psychological components have nevertheless remained relatively unelaborated, so that there is scope for the use of other, parallel models which present explanations amenable to gate control theory.

References

Bates, M.S. (1987) Ethnicity and pain: a biocultural model. *Social Science and Medicine*, 24: 47–50.

Beecher, H.K. (1959) *Measurement of Subjective Responses*. New York: Oxford University Press.

Boring, E.G. (1942) *Sensation and Perception in the History of Experimental Psychology*. New York: Appleton-Century-Crofts.

Ciccone, D.S. and Grzesiak, R.C. (1984) Cognitive dimensions of pain. *Social Science and Medicine*, 19: 1339–45.

Craig, K.D. (1984) Psychology of pain. *Postgraduate Medical Journal*, 60: 835–40.

Craig, K.D., Whitfield, M.F., Grunau, R.V. and Linton, J. (1993) Pain in the preterm neonate: behavioural and physiological indices. *Pain*, 52: 287–99.

Descartes, R. (1664) L'Homme, trans. M. Foster (1901), in *Lectures on the history of physiology during the 16th, 17th and 18th centuries*. Cambridge: Cambridge University Press.

Eccleston, C. (1995) The attentional control of pain: methodological and theoretical concerns. *Pain*, 63: 3–10.

Everson, S. (ed.) (1991) *Psychology*. Cambridge: Cambridge University Press.

Fordyce, W.E., Fowler, R.S., Lehmann, J.F. and DeLateur, B.J. (1968) Some implications of learning in problems of chronic pain. *Journal of Chronic Disorders*, 21: 179–90.

Gibson, S.J., Katz, B., Corran, T.M. and Farrell, M.J. (1994) Chronic and acute pain syndromes in patients with multiple sclerosis. *Acta Neurologica*, 16: 97–102.

Goldscheider, A. (1884) Die specifische Energie der Gefühlsnerven der Haut. *Monatsschrift für Praktische Dermatologie*, 3: 283–303.

Graham, G. (1993) *Philosophy of Mind*. Oxford: Blackwell.

Grahek, N. (1991) Objective and subjective aspects of pain. *Philosophical Psychology*, 4: 249–66.

Grounds, A. (1987) On describing mental states. *British Journal of Medical Psychology*, 60: 305–11.

Huxley, A. (1946) Limbo ('Cynthia'). London: Chatto & Windus.

Jacquette, D. (1985) Logical behaviorism and the simulation of mental episodes. *Journal of Mind and Behavior*, 6: 325–32.

Jensen, J. (1988) Pain in non-psychotic psychiatric patients: life events, symptomatology and personality traits. *Acta Psychiatrica Scandinavica*, 78: 201–7.

Kremer, E.F., Atkinson, J.H. and Kremer, A.M. (1983) The language of pain: affective descriptors of pain are a better predictor of psychological disturbance than pattern of sensory and affective descriptors. *Pain*, 16: 185–92.

Larbig, W. (1991) Gate control theory of pain perception: current status, in J.G. Carlson and A.R. Seifert (eds) *International Perspectives on Self-Regulation and Health*. New York: Plenum Press.

Lavigne, J.V., Schulein, M.J. and Hahn, Y.S. (1986) Psychological aspects of painful medical conditions in children. *Pain*, 27: 133–46.

Lewith, G.T. and Kenyon, J.N. (1984) Physiological and psychological explanations for the mechanism of acupuncture as a treatment in chronic pain. *Social Science and Medicine*, 19: 1367–78.

Livingston, W.K. (1943) *Pain Mechanisms*. New York: Macmillan.

Loeser, J.D. (1980) Low back pain, in J.J. Bonica (ed.) *Pain*. New York: Raven Press.

McMurray, G.A. (1975) Theories of pain and congenital universal insensitivity to pain. *Canadian Journal of Psychology*, 29: 302–15.

Malow, R.M. and Dougher, M.J. (1979) A signal detection analysis of the effects of transcutaneous stimulation on pain. *Psychosomatic Medicine*, 41: 101–8.

Melzack, R. (1993) Pain: past, present and future. *Canadian Journal of Experimental Psychology*, 47: 615–29.

Melzack, R. and Wall, P.D. (1965) Pain mechanisms: a new theory. *Science*, 150: 971–9.

Melzack, R. and Wall, P.D. (1982) *The Challenge of Pain*. Harmondsworth: Penguin.

Muller, J. (1842) *Elements of Physiology*. London: Taylor.

Niven, C.A. and Carroll, D. (eds) (1993) *The Health Psychology of Women*. Langhorne, PA: Harwood Academic.

Price, D.D., Rafii, A., Watkins, L.R. and Buckingham, B. (1984) A psychophysical analysis of acupuncture analgesia. *Pain*, 19: 27–42.

Prkachin, K.M. (1992) The consistency of facial expressions of pain: a comparison across modalities. *Pain*, 51: 297–306.

Rollman, G.B. (1992) Cognitive effects in pain and pain judgements, in D. Algom (ed.) *Psychophysical Approaches to Cognition*. Amsterdam: North Holland Elsevier Science.

Schneider, F. and Karoly, P. (1983) Conceptions of the pain experience: the emergence of multidimensional models and their implications for contemporary clinical practice. *Clinical Psychology Review*, 3: 61–86.

Shanfield, S.B. and Killingworth, R.N. (1977) The psychiatric aspects of pain. *Psychiatric Annals*, 7: 11–19.

Siegel, L.J. and Smith, K.E. (1989) Children's strategies for coping with pain. *Pediatrician*, 16: 110–18.

Sternbach, R.A. (1978) *Psychology of Pain*. New York: Raven Press.

Stevens, B. and Johnston, C.C. (1993) Pain in the infant: theoretical and conceptual issues. *Maternal Child Nursing Journal*, 21: 3–14.

Villaruel, A.M. (1995) Mexican–American cultural meanings, expressions, self-care and dependent-care actions associated with experiences of pain. *Research in Nursing and Health*, 18: 427–36.

von Frey, M. (1894) Beiträge zur Physiologie des Schmerzsinnes. Bericht über die Verhandlung der königlichen sächsisger Gesellschaft der Wissenschaften zu Leipzig, mathematisch-physiologische Klasse 46, 185–96 and 288–96.

Yang, Z.-L., Cai, T.-W. and Wu, J.-L. (1984) Psychological aspects of components of pain. *Journal of Psychology*, 118: 135–46.

Zatzick, D.F. and Dimsdale, J.E. (1990) Cultural variations in response to painful stimuli. *Psychosomatic Medicine*, 52: 544–57.

Zborowski, M. (1952) Cultural components in responses to pain. *Journal of Social Issues*, 8: 16–30.

Pain mechanisms

Future research on pain-modulating systems holds promise,
not only for greater understanding of variability in the pain
experience, but for significant advances in pain management.
(Larbig 1991)

Summary

Advances in our understanding of the physiology of pain response and
pain mechanisms appear to support the view that a physiological model is
insufficient. In fact, advances in this area have supported evidence for psychological, social and cultural factors by presenting potential physiological
correlates of these, although these still tend to be descriptive rather than
attempts to disprove hypotheses. As a more complete picture emerges, so
it becomes possible further to develop treatments and interventions, both
in an absolute sense and for the individual needs of patients. Finally, points
raised by the advent of gate control theory which remained controversial
or lacking in evidence, such as the role of descending factors in modulating pain response, have found significant recent support. In particular, the
isolation of endogenous opioids and evidence for central neural plasticity
associated with pain, in particular chronic pain, have been important steps
towards a more complete understanding of pain.

Introduction

The gate control theory to a large extent rejuvenated a field which had
become stagnant, particularly among clinicians who thought treatment
methods to be largely adequate and were only slightly concerned with the
development of theory. Even among more theoretical researchers the failure of existing specificity and patterning theories had led to a reluctance to
pursue these further. With the advent of a new theory came the opportunity to expand on the basic model and with this came an expansion in the
number of research projects dedicated to this area (Fields 1983). Reveal-
ingly, this expansion came not only from a range of biological and

physiological scientists, such as anatomists, biochemists and pharmaco-logists, but also from behavioural scientists such as psychologists; the expansion was in quality as well as quantity. It had become clear that pain was a phenomenon which could be understood fully only if several differ-ent approaches and models were incorporated at different levels; most importantly, it was increasingly accepted that behavioural and psychological factors were crucial to any complete model of pain. This multidisciplinary feature of pain research is one that has gained increasing acceptance, although there remain exceptions; the reductionist nature of modern science is to a large extent irreconcilable with pain phenomena for reasons already explored. While some advances have been made in further explaining the mechanisms of pain information transmission, in particular the site and nature of the gating mechanism, greater advances have been made in understanding the factors influencing pain information modulation and the mechanisms which underlie these. As will be seen, while these appear ini-tially to be advances in understanding the pharmacology and physiology of pain, the implications are in fact far broader. The three most important recent advances have been the identification of the neurotransmitter prim-arily responsible for the transmission of pain information, the isolation of endogenous morphine-like substances, which appear to act as a natural, self-regulatory pain control mechanism, and increasing evidence for central neural changes following peripheral tissue or nerve damage, which may explain certain pathological pain states, the genesis of which often remains unclear. It is interesting that the latter returns us to some degree to the work of pattern theorists before the advent of gate control theory. While these present a more complete physiological model of pain sensation, the real strength of these advances is in their ability to provide correlates for the psychological processes and factors known to modulate pain sensation. As our understanding advances, so it becomes clearer that various factors, rather than being distinct, are in fact fundamentally interdependent, reflect-ing different aspects of similar processes.

In the 1930s a neurotransmitter which did not behave as known trans-mitters was isolated by von Euler and Gaddum and became known as 'substance P' (Cuello and Matthews 1984). It was not until the 1950s that this peptide became known to be associated with sensory information trans-mission, and this has now been established as the primary neurotransmitter of pain information. Substance P is now regarded as the prototype for other peptides contained in peripheral sensory nerve fibres. This class of peptides, rather than substance P alone, is most probably responsible for conveying pain information to the CNS, but it is research on substance P which has proved most fruitful. In keeping with the suggestion made above, that the advent of gate control theory stimulated a new wave of multi-disciplinary research into all aspects of pain phenomena, the neurochemistry of substance P began to be known in detail only in the 1970s, for example in the work of Hokfelt and colleagues (Cuello and Matthews 1984) in demonstrating its existence in a wide variety of peripheral structures which interacted with substance P. It is now regarded as the most important neurotransmitter of sensory information, which includes information about painful stimulation as a subclass. Perhaps the most exciting advance in the physiology and biochemistry of pain mechanisms, certainly as far as providing a physiological correlate of psychological processes and adding detail to the concept of descending signals modulating pain sensation, came from research into another set of peptides: the endogenous opioids. This was followed more recently by evidence for plasticity in the central nervous system, in particular the possibility that peripheral nerve or tissue damage might sensitize spinal transmission pathways. The return to and further evolution of patterning theories appears to offer another piece of the puzzle. Taken as a whole, the detailed explication of the physiology of pain sensation, rather than denying the role of psychological factors or placing them on the periphery, has instead emphasized the importance of acknowledging the interaction of these with physiological and physical factors. The majority of advances in our understanding of the physiological mechanisms have contributed to a clearer picture of what form descending signals modulating pain sensation might take, and how psychological, social and cultural differences develop, perhaps in parallel. It is reasonable to suggest that a mechanism identified as responsible for the development of individual differences in pain response will also act at different scales (i.e. within cultures and across cultures), and that these differences may be describable with reference to both physiological and cognitive-behavioural models.

Endogenous opioids

Opioids, specifically opium, have been used for pain control at least since the reference to the uses of opium by Theophrastus in the third century BC. Nevertheless, it was not until the 1800s that Serturner isolated the active analgesic in opium and named it as morphine, after Morpheus, the Greek god of dreams. From this a powerful industry developed with a view to producing semi-synthetic derivatives from the morphine molecule and some entirely synthetic substances. The factors common to these compounds include, primarily, strong analgesic properties, as well as less desirable characteristics such as respiratory depression and physical dependence. Since none of the derivatives of morphine have been shown to be appreciably superior to morphine it is this which is regarded as the paradigmatic and prototypical analgesic in the opioid class. Broadly, results with reference to morphine can be generalized to other morphine-like substances, the opioids, and this also appears to be the case with endogenous opioids, which appear naturally as an internal pain-regulation system.

   Given the long history of opioids in medical use it is perhaps surprising that the mechanism by which these act, specifically at CNS sites, remained unclear until the late 1960s. The advance came with the simple realization that the effectiveness of opioid substances was due to the existence of an endogenous opioid system occurring naturally which was crucial to the mediation of pain sensation. The fact that morphine worked as an analgesic was simply due to the existence of structurally similar structures in human pain mechanisms which performed a functionally similar role, that is, the modulation of pain information transmission. Central receptors sensitive to morphine are those receptors which endogenous opioid peptides act on, producing similar if less intense effects. One important feature of opioid-induced analgesia is that it is selective, so that other modalities such as vision and audition are unaffected at therapeutic dosages. This is less surprising when it is understood that endogenous pain control exists, in that a generalized effect on other modalities would be unlikely to present an evolutionary advantage, so that there exists a self-regulatory system which provides limited analgesia when required by the organism. The caveat 'as required' is important in that the analgesia is situation dependent and difficult to stimulate; while endogenous opioid release has been proposed as a mechanism for the 'runner's high', whereby prolonged physical exertion results in a degree of analgesia and a sensation of well-being, there is evidence that this takes place only when activity at aerobic threshold is maintained for at least 20 minutes. It would be disadvantageous for a system to develop which readily provided a level of analgesia, simply because pain serves a valuable 'early-warning' role. Endogenous opioids, therefore, are released in strength only when the situation demands it, such as after extended physical exertion. The administration of, for example, morphine serves to bypass this endogenous self-regulation, which appears to have a clear effect on pain sensation only after an extreme exogenous event. The question, given the apparent difficulty in stimulating major release of endogenous opioids, is whether the existence of endogenous opioids can provide a potential mechanism by which descending CNS signals act on the gating mechanism.

Endogenous opioids were first isolated in the 1970s by Hughes and Kosterlitz (Hughes *et al.* 1975) in animal studies, and subsequently isolated in human subjects. There are currently understood to be at least three distinct populations of endogenous opioid-containing cells with different central distributions, incorporating five endogenous opioid peptides. These peptides are Leu-enkephalin, Met-enkephalin, B-endorphin, Dynorphin and A-neoendorphin. The specific action of these peptides is beyond the scope of this text, but the importance and role of the endogenous opioid system will be discussed below (pp. 21–6). That opioid subtypes exist, however, has motivated research concerned with the identification of receptor selective opioids and the manufacture of these. These synthetic opioids, while broadly acting as morphine, show reduced tolerance effects and respiratory depression. Moreover, tolerance that does develop appears to be receptor specific also (Gebhart 1991), so that individuals who require long-term narcotic analgesia can avoid many of the attendant risks of prolonged morphine use.

Investigating endogenous pain regulation

It is the analgesia produced by specific stimulation of certain brain sites, in humans an area of the midbrain, which gives an example of the role of endogenous opioids. The specificity of effect noted for opioid produced analgesia is present here also, in that most patients note no effects of stimulation other than analgesia and other modalities remain unaffected. It might be suggested that this area is important for the detection of pain information signals, and when stimulated this function is impacted upon. However, this cannot be the case as lesions to this area in animals appear not to impair pain information transmission; that is, pain behaviours remain apparently unaffected, although one must be careful not to state this too strongly. Two tentative conclusions can be drawn: if this brain site is crucial to pain sensation, the mechanism of action is mediated by endogenous opioid release and not direct functional inhibition; and, it is fair to assume that a comparable system exists in humans. The implication is that stimulation of this area causes active inhibition of pain information transmission at some other point, suggesting that central correlates of pain sensation mediate the release of endogenous opioids, thereby providing evidence for descending signals modulating pain sensation. This suggestion is reinforced by the finding that stimulation of these midbrain sites inhibits transmission at the site of the spinal cord, which indicates a descending pathway from brainstem to spinal cord mediating the pain suppression. Moreover, there exist several sites, including the sensory motor cortex and the internal capsule, which, when stimulated, result in a level of hyperalgesia. This has two implications: that the notion of one pain information reception site is misguided, and that there may exist an endogenous system for sensitizing the organism to painful stimulation. While stimulation of specific brain sites produces analgesia, a similar effect can be obtained from stimulation of peripheral sites, which also can be blocked by the administration of naloxone. Consequently, a further question is whether the analgesia produced by these two methods is the result of endogenous opioid release mediated by a single system, or whether central and peripheral endogenous opioid populations can be stimulated independently.

Given that much early research on the endogenous opioids was carried out in animals, it became important to demonstrate the existence of the system in humans, with an attendant increase in ethical and methodological issues. While it is common to isolate endogenous opioids in animals (although by no means straightforward), this is unappealing to most human subjects as it requires quite intrusive procedures such as direct access to cerebrospinal fluid. Unfortunately, direct measurement of endogenous opioid release is the only means by which strong evidence for the role of this mechanism in mediating a specific phenomenon can be achieved. Even this is potentially flawed as central and peripheral endogenous opioid action is not the same thing; notwithstanding this difficulty, the main problem in identifying a role for endogenous opioids in humans is the general preclusion of intrusive methods, so that alternative methodologies have had to be developed. Commonly, the experimental approach is to administer the opioid antagonist naloxone, used clinically to counter morphine overdose and subsequent respiratory depression. The rationale is that if, for example, the stimulation produced analgesia resulting from midbrain stimulation can be blocked by naloxone, this is evidence for an endogenous opioid-mediated system being responsible for the effect. Unfortunately there are attendant difficulties with this methodology, not least the fact that at different concentrations naloxone can act as an opioid agonist. More interesting is the finding that the analgesia-blocking effects of naloxone are closely correlated with the placebo responsiveness of subjects. If subjects are pooled into groups representing placebo responders and placebo non-responders, on the basis of a response to inert saline solution, for example, the effect of naloxone on blocking stimulation-produced analgesia becomes greater in the former group while disappearing in the latter (see Gibson *et al.* 1994). This presents the intriguing possibility that the placebo effect, where, for example, up to 30 per cent of chronic pain patients report equal pain relief from a masked inert saline injection as from a morphine injection (Wall 1984), may be an endogenous opioid mediated system, with placebo responders representing a subpopulation with a sensitive or highly developed endogenous opioid system. It has also been suggested that the efficacy of naloxone implies the existence of an endogenous substance with a similar opioid-antagonist action, with the function of regulating opioid release and action. That there exists a self-regulating system which modulates pain sensation and which can be stimulated by exogenous events, is well established; however, it is likely that at present only half of the mechanism is even slightly understood. Returning to methodological problems, it is also now clear that endogenous opioids exist in both central and peripheral populations, so that the site of action may remain unclear even if there is inductive evidence for their mediation of the phenomenon under investigation. As has been mentioned, this is difficult to resolve even if direct measurement of endogenous opioids is possible, and nearly impossible if the standard human methodology of naloxone administration is followed.

Experiments of this sort have also been used to provide evidence for the mechanism underlying the clinical effectiveness of acupuncture in pain control (Kraus 1977). While complementary treatments of this sort remained for a long time at the fringe of clinical medicine, acupuncture has recently gained considerable credence, not least because of its proven effectiveness in pain control, to the extent that palliative care doctors and general practitioners now suggest acupuncture to their patients. This position has been further strengthened by studies which report the blocking of acupuncture analgesia by naloxone (Lewith and Kenyon 1984), which again suggests a role for an endogenous opioid system. At this stage it is important to realize that the mechanism of acupuncture analgesia represents a more complex system than simply an endogenous opioid response to peripheral stimulation. Activity in peripheral A-delta and A-beta fibres simultaneously (carrying information about sharp pain and light touch respectively) has been shown to maximally inhibit transmission of C-fibre information (dull, throbbing pain) to the higher CNS (Lewith and Kenyon 1984). It appears, then, that acupuncture analgesia results from both the pattern of peripheral activity and descending signals from the endogenous opioid system, both acting to close the gate. This point is made to further emphasize the inter-active and synergistic nature of intrinsic pain modulation systems, and is probably true to a greater or lesser extent in all pain therapies. In the same way that physiological and psychological factors are now accepted to interact, so structural and pharmacological factors within a physiological model inter-act to modulate pain sensation. Pain therapies and interventions previously regarded as on the fringe of scientific medicine are now being understood in the context of gate control theory and interacting explanatory models, which establishes them with a certain academic and scientific popularity (however fairly or unfairly!).

This synergy is also apparent in the interaction of substance P and endo-genous opioid peptides (Hall and Stewart 1983). The variety of stressful pro-cedures which produce analgesia in animals (e.g. immobilization, footshock) appears to be mediated by an endogenous opioid system, in that the effect may be blocked by the administration of naloxone. Furthermore, footshock-induced analgesia is greatly reduced in morphine-tolerant subjects, which provides converging evidence. However, the endogenous opioid-mediated effects appear only when the shock is prolonged – for brief, intense shock the subsequent analgesia does not appear to be opioid in nature. Hall and Stewart also present evidence that the opioid shock-induced analgesia can be blocked by the administration of substance P, which is surprising in that administration of substance P in unstressed subjects produces a degree of analgesia. A possible explanation is that descending influences, following shock, inhibit substance P release, and that this can be reversed by exogen-ous administration of substance P. This does not occur for non-opioid shock-induced analgesia. Finally, it is reasonable to assume that broadly similar systems underlie the shock-induced analgesia phenomenon in human subjects, and we are consequently presented with an endogenous pain-control mechanism that relies on the interaction of a variety of endogenous substances. This itself is far removed from any specificity theory of pain information transmission; the physiology of endogenous pain modulation, then, has been shown so far to rely on one system dependent on the action of substance P, one system dependent on endogenous opioid action, and on the pattern of activation in peripheral nerve structures. Central neural changes, as will be seen, present yet another system, so that the interactivity of physiological factors alone is bewildering, before any attempt is made to integrate psychological, social and cultural factors.

It is important to realize, then, that studies using naloxone provide only indirect evidence that a function is mediated to some extent by an endogenous opioid system, and that endogenous opioids themselves are not the only substances modulating and regulating pain sensation: any complete model will have to incorporate what is known about endogenous opioids, substance P, and peripheral and central neural activity and plasticity. Alternative methodological approaches, to address the shortcomings of naloxone methodologies, may include a search for cross-tolerances between opioids and the analgesia manipulation concerned, such as the reduction in level of shock-induced analgesia in animal subjects with high levels of opioid tolerance (see p. 25), although there are unique ethical issues associated with adopting an approach of this sort with human subjects. Also, direct evidence may be achieved if endogenous opioids can be isolated concurrently with the production of, for example, stimulation produced analgesia. However, given the extent to which endogenous opioids act throughout the CNS, and the number of endogenous opioid types, there are limitations to this approach also. Cerebrospinal fluid concentration of endogenous opioids does not directly reflect the concentration at central sites, although the two are correlated. Finally, the fact that an endogenous opioid mechanism is implicated does not allow us to conclude that pain modulation is the primary function in this case. Aloisi *et al.* (1992), for example, present evidence that exploratory behaviour in rabbits is reduced when B-endorphin activity is blocked. The stimulation used to induce the behaviour was mildly painful, but there was evidence that this was not modulated by B-endorphin. The conclusion was that B-endorphin stimulated behaviour that was nonspecific to painful stimulation, which implies that at least this endogenous opioid has a role that is broader than simply pain modulation. This is likely to be true of any system implicated in the modulation of pain sensation, so that it is unlikely that a system dedicated to the modulation of pain will be found: the primary role of endogenous opioids appears to be the self-regulation of pain, but ancillary effects of endogenous opioid action appear to extend beyond this. The identification of such effects has indeed begun: Gebhart (1991) notes that the modulation of blood pressure is to an extent endogenous opioid-mediated following injury. This is clearly adaptive for the individual following tissue damage, so that endogenous opioids may be viewed in the broader context of acting to optimize the recovery of the injured organism.

The function of endogenous pain regulation

The importance of an endogenous pain regulation system is apparent, and the evolutionary advantage conveyed by this equally apparent. Furthermore, we are able to offer alternative or complementary explanations to those presented by, for example, Beecher (1959). Where the apparent indifference to pain in wounded soldiers was initially explained with reference to psychological factors such as relief to be away from the front line, we can now suggest that the physiological correlate of this is a release of endogenous opioids. Indeed, there is evidence that any major trauma is accompanied by a release of endogenous opioids, so that initially wounded soldiers may experience a comparable level of pain to wounded civilians, with differences only appearing at a later stage; although fewer civilian subjects with major trauma report lack of pain, the proportion is still considerable (*c.*30 per cent – p. 5). One point, raised here and elaborated in future sections, is that psychological factors may vary in importance over time, so that major physical trauma, for example, results in pain which can be explained in largely physiological terms. As the pain (and/or tissue damage) persists, so the opportunity for psychological factors to mediate pain sensation increases; while intuitively appealing, there is evidence, certainly in specific cases, that this is indeed part of the story. On a further methodological note, the self-regulatory nature of pain sensation modulation appears to be highly sensitive and delicate; administration of morphine or naloxone, or the induction of shock to central brain structures, is a rather crude means of determining the nature of the system acting. The nature of the methodologies used is likely to induce a degree of distortion in the system, and as such it will be possible to make only crude inferences.

It also appears that this pain regulation system is one that develops after birth, with Hamm and Knisely presenting evidence to this effect from animal studies (Hamm and Knisely 1984; 1985). In the study 10-day-old rats were shown to display less analgesia (as assessed by observation of pain behaviours) following shock than 28-day-old and 5–7-month-old rats, and further the administration of naloxone increased the analgesia in the 10-day-old rats, while blocking the analgesia fully in the 28-day-old rats and partially in the 5–7-month-old rats. This last observation was taken as evidence that non-opioid analgesia systems (cf. Hall and Stewart 1983) develop more slowly than opioid analgesia systems. Subsequent findings indicate that at the other end of the lifespan the function of endogenous pain regulatory systems declines with age, and that this is accompanied by a generalized reduction in responsiveness to opioid substances. Whether this has clear implications for theory and practice in human subjects remains to be established, but it is an issue which must be addressed by those hoping to provide adequate pain control in the young and in elderly people, given that the mechanisms by which interventions act may be at a different level of development to those in individuals on whom the interventions were initially tested and validated.

The extent to which endogenous opioids mediate pain information transmission is great, even if the specifics of this action remain unclear, and it is factors such as these which represent the 'descending signals' incorporated by Melzack and Wall (1982) in their theory. At least there is now the opportunity to suggest a specific mechanism by which, for example, anxiety may sensitize an individual to painful stimulation. However, this does not mean that endogenous opioids present the only mechanism by which descending signals are mediated, or that pain modulation is their only function (cf. Aloisi *et al.* 1992). For some time the notion of pain 'memories' (Coderre *et al.* 1993) has suggested a role for structural factors in the CNS in mediating pain information transmission. Phantom limb pain and an extensive literature on other painful and non-painful sensations which persist after the removal or deafferentation of associate body parts other than limbs provides evidence in support of the notion that peripheral tissue or nerve damage can lead to higher CNS changes associated with pathological pain states. It is not until the 1990s, however, that a description of this mechanism has begun to be explicated. While endogenous opioid systems (as well as those mediated by substance P and patterns of peripheral neural activity) appear to be of primary importance in normal subjects, central, structural factors seem to play a crucial role in determining the development and maintenance of pathological pain states.

Central neural plasticity

Certainly the suggestion that peripheral injury may result in altered CNS function and, in turn, altered pain sensitivity, is by no means new. In the 1880s Sturge proposed the existence of an increase in CNS sensitivity following peripheral injury, resulting in hypersensitivity to painful stimulation (Coderre *et al.* 1993). A decade later MacKenzie (1893) made a similar suggestion, proposing the spinal cord as the structure where this sensitivity 'focused'. This idea of hypersensitivity of CNS structures, frequently supposed to be at the site of the spinal cord, continued in varying forms through the twentieth century, with the common feature that none of the hypotheses suggested were accompanied by empirical evidence and instead relied wholly on description. It was not until the late 1970s that these suggestions began to be supported to some degree by empirical results, with the demonstration that noxious peripheral stimulation produced changes in the sensitivity of dorsal horn neurons to further stimulation (Coderre *et al.* 1993). These results, however, reflected relatively transient changes, and it was not until the 1980s that evidence pertaining to sustained changes in central excitability was presented, with important demonstrations such as that by Woolf (Coderre *et al.* 1993) who showed that increases in spinal cord excitability following noxious stimulation could be maintained even after local anaesthesia at the site of injury.

It is an understanding of the pathological pain states, described briefly in the introduction, which evidence of this nature may aid. While the original gate control theory proposed that these pain states could potentially be accounted for with reference to alterations in the CNS mediation of pain information transmission, specific evidence was not available at that time to suggest what form such a mechanism might take. Recently, however, evidence concerning the plasticity of CNS structures has provided an indication as to the details of this mechanism.

Dubner and Ruda (1992) review the evidence that tissue injury results in the increased sensitivity of peripheral neurons, taking the form of spontaneous activity, lowered thresholds, and increased responsiveness to noxious stimuli. This appears to sit comfortably with behavioural changes accompanying tissue injury, in particular in cases of pathological pain, where pain can occur spontaneously or following stimulation by an apparently innocuous stimulus. These cases of spontaneous pain and hyperalgesia (excessive sensitivity to pain) appear to be the result of changes in the spinal dorsal horns and medullary receiving input from these peripheral sites. It is revealing that the mechanisms suggested at the end of the nineteenth century do in fact appear to exist, albeit not exactly in the form originally envisaged. Pathological pain states seem, at least in part, to be the result of structural and organic changes, so that the pathology may be regarded as organic. As will be discussed in later sections, however, this is unlikely to offer a complete explanation – in particular, the evidence from behavioural and psychological treatment programmes suggests an important role for these factors in at least a subgroup of pathological pain states, with recent evidence that these factors are closely related to the structural changes detailed here. The evidence for strong psychological factors mediating these states, and the possibility of the interaction of physical and psychological factors will be explored. At this stage it is sufficient to note that, regardless of the evidence presented in the introduction that simple mechanistic models of pain are likely to be inadequate, it is still often assumed that apparent anomalies in pain phenomena can be explained with reference to a more completely elaborated physiological model.

The mechanism by which pain information transmission may lead to central neural changes is further explored by Dickenson (1991). What is important in this review is that changes at both spinal and peripheral sites are suggested, and furthermore that there is an interaction between 'excitatory amino acids, opioids, monoamines and non-opioid peptides', which may persist for several days following injury. This is not included here to suggest a comprehensive review of the physiological substrate of central plasticity phenomena, but instead to emphasize the interactive complexity of any theory which hopes to approach adequacy. For example, there is evidence that opioid mechanisms exhibit plasticity themselves (Lipman *et al.* 1990), so that pathological pain states may not only be the result of functional and structural changes in neuron sensitivity. The scope of plasticity phenomena, in both CNS and peptide systems, in the mediation of pain sensation is unclear, and there remains the question of to what extent these changes are related to attendant behavioural and psychological changes.

To what extent these neural changes are related to pathological pain states remains a question of crucial importance (Melzack and Loeser 1978), given that it is the behavioural expression of pain which is the ultimate criterion in determining the existence of pain (cf. Wittgenstein 1963). Further, it is phenomena such as spontaneous pain and hyperalgesia which provided the impetus for change which ultimately resulted in the widespread adoption of the gate control theory of pain. Consequently, one test of the superiority of the new theory is its ability to explain these phenomena in an adequate, testable way. While it has already been noted that the idea of central changes resulting in pathological pain states is not a new one (Coderre *et al.* 1993), the use of empirical evidence in support of these and similar suggestions is recent. Woolf's finding that injury-induced changes in spinal-cord excitability could be maintained after the site of injury had been anaesthetized was crucial in this (Woolf 1983). Furthermore, Woolf and Wall (1986) showed that ten times as much morphine was required to reverse this hyperexcitability as was required to prevent its establishment (Coderre *et al.* 1993). As well as increased sensitivity there is evidence that peripheral damage can lead to the expansion of the receptive fields of spinal neurons, which goes further in explaining the behavioural phenomena in pathological pain states such as pain following stimulation at a site other than that of the original injury. The growing interest in this field, stimulated by the theoretical and clinical importance of the findings, has led to the development of several detailed theories of how noxious stimuli produce these changes in CNS function.

While these findings go a long way to explaining the phenomena observed in pathological pain states, there is still a grossly inadequate understanding of the transition from normal to pathological pain. To an extent this is the result of a continuance of a simple, dichotic conception of pain as either acute or chronic, with the former being regarded as in some sense 'normal'. In the same way that physiological and psychological factors can now be integrated in any model of pain, there is a need for acute and chronic dimensions to be assimilated more completely, an issue to be discussed in more detail in later sections. The question, then, is why we do not all develop some level of persistent or chronic pain after injury. Two possible explanations offer themselves from the material reviewed so far: one is that the relative reduction in quantity of C-fibres compared to A-delta fibres disrupts the self-regulatory mechanism of peripheral neural activity, a contention supported by evidence that this relative reduction does in fact take place following peripheral nerve damage (Melzack and Wall 1982); another possible explanation is that persistent pain from some physical pathology which resolves only slowly presents the opportunity for central neural changes to occur, where sufficient duration is required for this to take place. This second explanation, in particular, suggests ways in which physiological and psychological explanation may overlap, as will be outlined on pp. 57–64. The issue is confounded by a lack of clarity in distinguishing persistent, chronic and pathological pain states, so that burns patients experience pain over an extended period but in a qualitatively different way from low back pain patients with no discernible physical pathology. Regarding the first explanation, that alterations in the distribution of peripheral nerve fibre types plays a role, Melzack and Wall (1982) have argued that in the case of causalgia, the neuralgias, and possibly phantom limb pain, the associated pathological pain is more likely to exist after partial deafferentation of peripheral nerve structures rather than after total destruction. Again, this suggests a role for structural factors.

There is consequently an issue regarding the degree to which these findings have a direct clinical application, and to what extent they may be assimilated with attempts to delineate the psychological factors modulating pathological pain states. The latter will be discussed in subsequent chapters, but regarding the former, salient clinical examples include phantom limb pain and chronic pain without discernible physical pathology, as well as the less common states such as causalgia and the neuralgias. For example, in the case of phantom limb pain, a major determinant of whether this results following amputation is whether pain in the limb is adequately controlled before the amputation is performed. This is supported, for example, by the evidence of Woolf and Wall that it requires less morphine to prevent the establishment of hypersensitivity in spinal neurons than to reverse this once it is established.

The most significant consequence of these results is that it becomes apparent that we must regard pain mechanisms as active systems which can be modified by past experiences and social learning, with social and cultural factors also playing a role at another level of explanation. Indeed, Melzack and Wall (1982) refer to 'memory-like systems' in pain, so that the neural mechanisms subserving long-term memory of sensory experiences will most probably play a major role in modulating pain response. Therefore, sensory stimuli input on neural systems that are constantly being modified as a result of this input; furthermore, these modifications act not only at the site of the neuron but also result in specific cellular and molecular changes, influencing membrane excitability and inducing new gene expression (Coderre et al. 1993). These changes may be the result of either or both descending and ascending signals, both of which modulate initial pain response (Melzack and Wall 1982). As a result of this conceptual shift, the acceptance that pathological pain states are correlated with central changes following peripheral injury has revealed an array of sites and mechanisms which are so influenced. While these results may provide future directions for pharmacological methods of pain control superior to those which already exist, there is perhaps more scope for the assimilation of behavioural and psychological interventions, as well as the refinement of procedure so that, for example, a patient's pain is adequately controlled before the amputation is performed, thereby greatly reducing the risk of phantom limb pain. The philosophical advance, however, is away from the 'hard-wired' system envisaged since Descartes (Randich 1993), and towards a fluid, active system which incorporates 'attentional, cognitive, motivational and emotional factors'. The identification of how these factors influence pain response presents an opportunity in itself, and some attendant methodological questions.

Conclusion

Further light has been shed on the role of 'descending factors' in the modulation of pain with the isolation and analysis of the endogenous opioid system and other peptides, notably substance P. It is also apparent that these peptides perform other functions than simply the self-regulation of pain response, and seem to enjoy a broader range of behavioural influences than was first anticipated. It is perhaps most accurate to represent the endogenous opioid system as influencing the survival value of the organism, of which pain regulation is an essential feature. Evidence for central neural plasticity following peripheral stimulation also has begun to make more concrete the assertions borrowed largely from patterning theories. A role for these factors in pathological pain states, in particular chronic pain states, suggests possible avenues for the further integration of psychological, behavioural and physiological explanatory models.

References

Aloisi, A.M., Panerai, A.E. and Carli, G. (1992) Nociceptive induced activation of exploratory behaviour: a role for B-endorphin. *Medical Science Research*, 20: 25–6.

Beecher, H.M. (1959) *Measurement of Subjective Responses*. New York: Oxford University Press.

Coderre, T.J., Katz, J., Vaccaino, A.L. and Melzack, R. (1993) Contribution of central neuroplasticity to pathological pain. *Pain*, 52: 259–85.

Cuello, A.C. and Matthews, M.R. (1984) Peptides in peripheral sensory nerve fibres, in P.D. Wall and R. Melzack (eds) *Textbook of Pain*. New York: Churchill Livingstone.

Dickenson, A.H. (1991) Recent advances in the physiology and pharmacology of pain: plasticity and its implications for clinical analgesia. *Journal of Psychopharmacology*, 5: 342–51.

Dubner, R. and Ruda, M.A. (1992) Activity-dependent neuronal plasticity following tissue injury and inflammation. *Trends in Neurosciences*, 15: 96–103.

Fields, H.L. (1983) Recent advances in research on pain and analgesia. *National Institute on Drug Abuse Research Monograph Series*, 45: 3–18.

Gebhart, G.F. (1991) Opioid analgesia and descending systems of pain control, in J.G. Carlson and A.R. Seifert (eds) *International Perspectives on Self-Regulation and Health*. New York: Plenum Press.

Gibson, S.J., Katz, B., Corran, T.M. and Socci, L. (1994) Pain in older persons. *Disability and Rehabilitation*, 16: 127–39.

Hall, M.E. and Stewart, J.M. (1983) Prevention of stress-induced analgesia by substance P. *Behavioural Brain Research*, 10: 375–82.

Hamm, R.J. and Knisely, J.S. (1984) Developmental changes in environmentally induced analgesia. *Developmental Brain Research*, 14: 93–9.

Hamm, R.J. and Knisely, J.S. (1985) Environmentally induced analgesia: an age-related decline in an endogenous opioid system. *Journal of Gerontology*, 40: 268–74.

Hughes, J., Smith, T.W. and Kosterlitz, H.W. (1975) Identification of two related pentapeptides from the brain with potent opioid agonist activity. *Nature*, 258: 577–9.

Kraus, H. (1977) Triggerpoints and acupuncture. *Acupuncture and Electro Therapeutics Research*, 2: 323–8.

Larbig, W. (1991) Gate control theory of pain perception: current status, in J.G. Carlson and A.R. Seifert (eds) *International Perspectives on Self-Regulation and Health*. New York: Plenum Press.

Lewith, G.T. and Kenyon, J.N. (1984) Physiological and psychological explanations for the mechanism of acupuncture as a treatment for chronic pain. *Social Science and Medicine*, 19: 1367–78.

Lipman, J.J., Miller, B.E., Mays, K.S. and Miller, M.N. (1990) Peak B-endorphin concentration in cerebrospinal fluid: reduced in chronic pain patients and increased during the placebo response. *Psychopharmacology*, 102: 112–16.

Melzack, R. and Loeser, J.D. (1978) Phantom body pain in paraplegics: evidence for a central 'pattern generating mechanism' for pain. *Pain*, 4: 195–210.

Melzack, R. and Wall, P.D. (1982) *The Challenge of Pain*. Harmondsworth: Penguin.

Randich, A. (1993) Neural substrates of pain and analgesia. *Arthritis Care and Research*, 6: 171–7.

Wall, P.D. (1984) Introduction, in P.D. Wall and R. Melzack (eds) *Textbook of Pain*. New York: Churchill Livingstone.

Wittgenstein, L.J.J. (1963) *Philosophical Investigations*, trans. G.E.M. Anscombe. Oxford: Blackwell.

Woolf, C.J. (1983) Evidence for a central component of post-injury pain hypersensitivity. *Nature*, 306: 686–8.

Woolf, C.J. and Wall, P.D. (1986) Morphine-sensitive and morphine-insensitive actions of C-fibre input on the rat spinal column. *Neuroscience Letters*, 64: 221–5.

CHAPTER
3

Laboratory studies

The delight of psychophysicists is their ability to establish thresholds of sensation and to measure lawful relations between stimulus intensity and the strength of sensation. They have obviously been very successful in vision and hearing. No such psychophysics exist for sensations such as hunger or thirst but there have been persistent attempts to establish thresholds and scales relating experimental stimuli to evoked pain.

(Wall 1979: 255)

Summary

The identification of the physiological mechanisms of pain response has proceeded, to a great extent, as a result of psychophysical studies on pain induced experimentally in the laboratory, with confounding factors held nominally constant. As psychological factors began to be accepted as crucial to any understanding of pain, there began an attempt to vary these systematically and thereby quantify their effect. The extent to which this has been successful, and is even possible, is discussed, with references to advances made in our theoretical understanding of pain and our effective treatment of it. The lack of integration of many of these studies perhaps lies in the difficulties associated with formulating testable hypotheses regarding psychological, social and behavioural factors from gate control theory.

Introduction

The distinction between the subjective experience of pain and its objective, behavioural and physiological correlates is not as clear as those influenced by the Cartesian conception of pain would suggest. While it is misleading to regard the physical and psychological mechanisms of pain sensation as separate, there is nevertheless scope to investigate one mechanism in isolation, attempting thereby to gain insight into the phenomenon as a whole. Caution is necessary if there is any attempt at reductionism, but when the whole is as subtle and complex as the pain mechanism is, it becomes important to reduce the problem to manageable proportions. To this end, there is an extensive literature which attempts to reduce the variability in factors influencing pain sensation by presenting painful stimuli to subjects in a laboratory environment. Much of the evidence referred to in the introduction regarding the physiology of pain mechanisms was arrived at using these methods, and while the simplistic models developed as a result of these findings have been shown to be inadequate, many of the findings remain valid. Rather than discarding existing evidence, the development of gate control theory required the incorporation of established results, as previously described. This chapter will outline the rationale behind laboratory studies of pain, and notable successes which have been achieved, as well as outlining the limitations of this approach.

The genesis of psychology as a science owes a great deal to the assumption that the human body is essentially a machine, albeit an infinitely complex and subtle one. At the same time as Mary Shelley was writing *Frankenstein* (1818), physiologists were attempting to relate the mechanics of the human body to attendant experiental phenomena. This came about in a cultural climate where it was claimed by the US Patent Office that everything which could be invented had been invented; Newtonian mechanics was supposed to offer the opportunity for all phenomena, including sensation and perception, to be explained and replicated. In this way, psychophysics was born, and rapidly assimilated into the nascent discipline of psychology. It was not until the careful research of Hardy and his colleagues in the 1940s, however, that human pain phenomena and the measurement of these were systematically investigated (Wolff 1977). Early research focused on sensory perception, particularly visual and auditory perception, and this perhaps suggests the beginnings of the assumption that pain is a perceptual process, an assumption which has arguably led to a degree of confusion. In summarizing the development of laboratory pain research, Hardy, Wolff and Goodell (Wolff 1977) outlined seven prerequisites for any adequate investigation of the phenomenon:

- the measurable aspect of the stimulus should be closely associated with changes causing pain, i.e. noxious stimulation
- the stimulus should be one for which, under the same conditions, reproducible quantitative measurements of the pain threshold are obtained
- the intensity of the stimulus should be controllable and measurable to a degree higher than the difference between two stimuli which evoke a just noticeable difference (JND) in pain sensation
- the stimulus should be one for which the ability of the subject to discriminate differences in pain intensity can be ascertained throughout the effective range of the stimulus, i.e. from the threshold to 'ceiling' pain
- the stimulus should cause minimal tissue damage at pain threshold and should be a minor hazard to the subject even at highest intensities
- the stimulus should be capable of evoking separately one of the qualities of pain – burning, pricking, aching

♦ the stimulus should be one for which the perception and identification of pain is clear cut, whether or not other sensations are evoked prior to, concomitant with, or following the pain.

This list is revealing in that it contains exemplars of both the strengths and weaknesses of this approach. For example, that tissue damage should be a necessary condition for the laboratory induction of pain is narrow sighted and, possibly, ethically questionable. Indeed, one of the authors of the list, Woolf (1977: 273), has identified this as a weakness of the list: 'it is not acceptable that tissue damage is a sine qua non for pain'. That tissue damage is neither a necessary nor sufficient condition for pain has been discussed at length in the introduction. Beecher (1959) adds four more requirements:

♦ the possibility of carrying out several to many repetitions of the stimulation even above the pain threshold value without interfering with subsequent determinations
♦ sensitivity so that agents of low analgesic power can be detected
♦ differentiation among graded doses of analgesic through their power to alter the effects of a standard pain stimulus
♦ applicability both to humans and to animals.

Again, these highlight the assumptions and very specific requirements attending research of this kind. That results should apply to both humans and animals requires the assumption that the fundamentals of any pain mechanism are, to a degree at least, universal to a range of species. This may be true to an extent, but when one accepts that psychological factors can mediate pain sensation it becomes difficult to generalize results supporting this to other species; what role can we attribute to anxiety in animal studies? Indeed, although we may want to attribute affective states to animals, metaphorically or otherwise, there are problems enough in attempting to investigate these systematically in humans. The point has already been made that any purely mechanistic conception of pain transmission and sensation, however complex and comprehensive, will be inadequate because it will address the phenomenon at only one level of explanation. Given these limitations, however, modern laboratory studies of pain proceed with one or both of two objectives: to further understand the physiological substrate of pain information transmission, or to make comparisons with findings achieved in a more ecological environment and thereby validate them. If a clear understanding of the limitations of this approach is maintained, there exists a potential to bring together different levels of explanation, for example by suggesting physiological correlates of psychological factors, so that laboratory studies are one valuable research tool in the arsenal of pain researchers.

Methodologies used

The historical influence of psychophysics is apparent in the terminology used in laboratory pain studies, dealing primarily with the relation between the physical stimulus and consequent sensory response. This sensory response is classically defined with reference to three parameters: pain threshold is defined as the minimal stimulus intensity perceived as painful; pain tolerance is the point at which the individual terminates the stimulation; pain endurance (or sensitivity range) represents the difference between tolerance and threshold. Commonly stimulation is increased incrementally, so that difference thresholds can also be established (just noticeable difference or JND), these being the smallest increase in stimulation intensity required for the subject to report a change in sensation. Again, this parallels the original interest of psychophysics in determining the quietest auditory stimulus which could be heard, for example, and neglects to a great extent the reason for a pain mechanism existing in the first place, and the function it serves in the broader context of a complete organism. There is a certain debate regarding the distinction between the status of pain as either a perceptual or sensory process (the two are by no means identical, or even similar), and pain as a need state (Wall 1983). The latter perhaps is more valid in that it acknowledges the function of pain and hints at the reason why advantage may have been gained by its evolution, but this validity may be at the expense of ease of systematic investigation (hunger is not a popular area of psychophysics). Nevertheless, the suggestion has been made previously that certain systems responsible for the mediation of pain response are perhaps better regarded in the broader context of ensuring the survival or the organism (cf. endogenous opioids and blood pressure control). This extends to the role of pain itself, as being in a sense a warning system; this suggestion is by no means novel, but evidence regarding the scope of systems subsuming pain response beyond pain alone presents a fresh perspective on this. The implicit assumption that pain is a perceptual process is one which leads to a degree of philosophical confusion and renders difficult any direct clinical application, since this necessarily requires an acceptance of the functional role of pain; a perceptual model of pain, however, can be described in isolation (more comparable to, for example, computational models of vision), and this should be regarded as a weakness. It is perhaps revealing that an acceptance of the need for pain research findings to be generalizable to ecological settings has led to the inclusion of the drug request point as another parameter in laboratory research. This is the degree of stimulation at which the individual would normally seek pain medication, and is of most interest to those concerned with treatment effects.

The induction of pain can also take one of several different forms, and requires a balance to be struck between the ethical considerations attending the induction of pain in subjects, whether human or animal, and the theoretical considerations concerning the validity of the pain induction method.

The extent to which mild laboratory pain is comparable to, say, pain in advanced cancer patients is questionable to say the least. This is not simply an issue regarding the intensity of the pain itself: given the emphasis placed on psychological and social factors thus far, it has to be realized that the cognitive and emotional issues attending cancer pain will be very different from those attending laboratory pain. Broadly speaking there are four methods of pain induction: thermal, electrical, chemical and mechanical. Thermal methods may include painful heat or painful cold, with the cold pressor technique (where the subject's hand, for example, is immersed in ice water) being a common example of the latter. Electrical methods are common, largely because of the ease with which they may be employed and the quantifiability of the stimulus. Chemical methods utilize chemical stimulation at varying tissue depths (e.g. cutaneous, subcutaneous, intraperitoneal and intramuscular), and can include ischaemic methods as the pain attending this is caused by resulting chemical changes. Finally, mechanical methods tend to use pressure, applied in various ways, although perhaps the simplest method, pinpricks, is inappropriate because of the difficulty in quantifying the stimulus.

Laboratory pain and development of theory

Laboratory pain induction methods represent an attempt to incorporate the individual's response in any investigation of pain mechanism, being important in that they require living, responsive subjects. In this sense they occupy a sometimes uncomfortable but nevertheless important position between purely physiological investigations of the mechanisms of pain sensation and psychological investigations of the factors modulating this sensation. That they can therefore provide insights into the mechanisms of pain sensation is perhaps surprising, then, since it is tempting to regard data from laboratory studies as in a sense providing baseline information in a controlled environment. The rationale underpinning laboratory studies is that factors which mediate pain response can be held constant and the effects of a single factor thereby isolated; to an extent, then, this denies the ecological environment altogether. What must be remembered is that pain mechanisms, rather than being passive, receptive systems, are active and designed to prompt action in response to stimulation that signals damage or danger, either current or impending. This action, which usually takes the form of an attempt to take evasive action or seek treatment, is what defines pain as a need state, in the same way that hunger is evidenced by verbal complaint, search for food, and so on. This active feature of pain response raises the question of whether it is possible to hold factors constant at all: given the highly individual nature of pain response, the laboratory environment may be one to which different individuals react very differently, thereby introducing a confounding factor.

There exists a bewildering array of material and evidence which attempts to delineate with an increasing degree of specificity the role of various factors in the mediation of, for example, pain threshold. A subgroup of these studies present evidence which can be incorporated in theoretical models of pain, rather than being largely descriptive in nature. A typical review in this area is provided by Albe-Fessard and Fessard (1975: 715) which, rather than being particularly revolutionary or seminal, emphasizes the advances in theory which can be prompted by laboratory studies of pain and attendant phenomena: 'Our paper aims at presenting a rapid survey of the most recent advances on the neuroanatomical and neurophysiological bases of pain sensation, with a relative emphasis given to work done in the laboratory'. For example, the high degree of specificity which exists in peripheral nerve structures has been demonstrated by the finding that certain fibres, both myelinated and unmyelinated, convey noxious information only. It is now commonly accepted that A-delta (myelinated) fibres carry information about sharp, brief pain, while C-fibres (unmyelinated) carry information about dull, throbbing pain. These differences in myelination, and subsequent transmission velocity, may account for such observed behavioural phenomena as secondary pain, where the initial pain of injury is followed shortly after by duller pain. Such studies to delineate the physiology of the peripheral sensory nervous system have been carried out on animals (where noxious stimulation is commonly referred to, rather than painful stimulation, although this distinction has recently weakened) and humans.

Other attempts to delineate the factors which must be incorporated in any adequate model of pain include attempts to correlate responses to noxious stimuli across modalities. In other words, is a subject's response to noxious heat stimulation related to his response to noxious ischaemic stimulation? This is of particular importance if one is concerned about the possibility of a 'pain-prone personality' existing, this being an individual more likely to exhibit pain behaviour for any given level of noxious stimulation. The existence of such a personality construct would imply that the effect was global, acting across all modalities of noxious stimulation, although failure to demonstrate this would by no means be catastrophic. The existing literature fails to provide conclusive evidence in either direction for the existence of such a correlation of response. Janal *et al.* (1994) present negative evidence, which the authors themselves offset with a discussion of other, equally recent studies that show a consistent correlation of about 0.50 across modalities. One suggestion made by the authors for this apparent incongruity is the extent to which laboratory studies may differ: for example, the stimulus may increase continuously, or remain constant with variation instead being over time. This highlights the difficulties associated with laboratory studies: the features of laboratory studies which are intended to be desirable (highly specific delineation of experimental variables) mean that it becomes increasingly difficult to compare results across studies which use even slightly different research paradigms; indeed, it may be fruitless to attempt such a comparison, given the number of factors held to be of importance. To be fair, this is a difficulty in all pain research given the extent to which pain phenomena are modulated by an array of other factors.

Another role which research of this kind may play is in determining whether the same peripheral nervous system is responsible for the transmission of noxious stimulation across modalities. Croze and Duclaux (1978), for example, investigate the relationship between pain threshold and pain tolerance. What is interesting for our current discussion is the finding that both heat stimulation and cold stimulation lead to similar results, which supports a global pain information transmission system, rather than unique systems for different sensory modalities. There is specificity for pain response systems, therefore, but not such a degree of specificity that pain from thermal stimulation, say, is subsumed by a different system to pain from mechanical stimulation.

While these studies provide clues as to the peripheral mechanisms of pain, there is also scope for central mechanisms to be investigated in this way. Neri *et al.* (1985) present evidence that brain damage influences responses to pain as measured by pain threshold and tolerance. These values were shown to be consistently and significantly higher for the paralysed limb following brain damage than for the contralateral limb. In normal subjects right-side body measurements were consistently lower than left-side body measurements for threshold and tolerance measures. Furthermore an effect was noted for the side on which the brain damage existed: left-brain damage was related to an inversion of the pattern found in normal subjects, while right-brain damage was related to an accentuation of it. Damage to the right-brain resulted in both arms being affected, whereas left-brain damage influenced only responses in contralateral measurements. The authors suggest that this is related to the role of the right hemisphere in mediating negative emotional experiences. This is revealing in that it implicitly suggests a role for an affective component in pain. This follows earlier work by Cubelli *et al.* (1984) which found that pain endurance (the difference between threshold and tolerance) was significantly elevated in right-side brain damaged patients compared to normal controls and left-side brain damaged patients. The converging evidence appears to point to the right hemisphere as playing a specific role in modulating pain sensation, indeed possibly all sensation, perhaps at an affective level, with laboratory studies presenting an opportunity to investigate the alterations in pain response following brain damage so that conclusions about normal function can be drawn.

Finally, the research motivated by the development of the gate control theory has to an extent ignored implications of the theory not directly related to pain sensation. The interaction between activity in different fibres acting to close the gate has focused on, for example, light touch inhibiting pain sensation (rubbing an injured area, for example, can reduce the pain of the injury). Apkarian *et al.* (1994) present evidence that an opposite interaction also exists: painful stimulation results in the inhibition of other sensation such as touch. The conclusion is that heat stimuli (as used in their study) capable of inducing pain can diminish tactile sensitivity to a significant degree. The authors conclude that this provides tentative evidence for the existence of a 'touch gate' comparable to that proposed by the gate control theory for pain. Quite how evidence such as this can be incorporated into existing models is unclear, but this goes a long way in emphasizing the interactive nature of all sensory and perceptual processes. With the majority of research focusing on the role of pain information transmission, the extent to which other sensory information is modulated by painful stimulation has been neglected. Once again, the scope of pain response mechanisms appears to be far broader than first imagined.

The broader scope of laboratory studies

These studies present a very brief overview of the questions which can, at least in principle, be answered by laboratory studies, and indeed the further questions which they can generate. Findings such as these present evidence which must be incorporated in any adequate model of pain sensation, and indeed any model of sensation in general. Laboratory studies, however, also present more descriptive findings where the extent to which it is possible, or indeed desirable, to incorporate these into physiological models of pain is questionable. These studies tend to delineate the psychological, social and behavioural variables which mediate pain response, and as such operate at an entirely different level of explanation, serving to answer an entirely different set of questions.

An example is the difference in pain threshold and, more significantly tolerance, which is exhibited between athletes and non-athletes (Jaremko *et al.* 1981). Various possible explanations for this exist: a physiological model might postulate an enhanced endogenous opioid system in athletes, possibly resulting from increased levels of training and subsequent ease of opioid release; alternatively, a cognitive-behavioural model might suggest cognitive coping strategies which have been developed by athletes to allow the maintenance of high levels of performance; finally, a radical behavioural model (that adopted by the authors in the Jaremko *et al.* study) might propose that pain response, both verbal and behavioural, is learned in relation to contingencies associated with painful stimulation (such as receipt of attention following pain report). The cognitive-behavioural approach is one adopted by many sports psychologists in their attempts to elicit still greater performances from their subjects, while the radical-behavioural perspective has motivated the development of treatment programmes reliant on an operant conditioning model, to be discussed in later chapters.

Other studies have attempted to relate pain and pain report to personality constructs (not necessarily the same thing, as personality may influence either pain response or the extent to which this is verbalized, or both). The notion of a pain-prone personality has already been discussed, but pain report may be related to well established personality constructs such as extraversion. Jamner *et al.* (1986) rated normal subjects using the Lie Scale of the Eysenck Personality Inventory, thereby classifying subjects as Low, Medium or High Deceptors. While there were no differences among groups on sensation threshold measures, pain threshold and tolerance levels, as well as ratings of discomfort, differed between Low and High Deceptor groups, with the latter apparently being able to endure higher levels of noxious stimulation. This highlights one fairly consistent finding which is that predictable differences across individuals tend to be on measures of the affective nature of pain, such as the unpleasantness of the stimulation, the point at which it becomes unpleasant, and so on. This perhaps should not be surprising, given that psychological factors will almost inevitably be more important along affective rather than purely sensory dimensions, further emphasizing the dissociation of these two components of pain.

One individual characteristic which can be assessed absolutely (with one or two rare exceptions) is the sex of the subject. The literature on the effects of sex (a between groups difference) and menstrual phase (within group) dates from the work of Herren in the 1930s (Goolkasian 1985). It appears that women's ability to respond to stimulation as pain varies as a function of menstrual cycle, with oral contraception acting to stabilize these responses. When oral contraception is taken, and pain responses subsequently stabilized, the pain response of women to a given stimulus is very similar to men. However, when phase effects are not stabilized in this way, differences appear between men and women, largely as a result of these phase effects: pain thresholds appear to be at a minimum during ovulation, rising to a maximum during menstruation. These effects do not appear to be the result of response bias alone. This suggests a physiological mechanism, and work on maternal rats indicates that this mechanism might be mediated by endogenous opioids: elevated pain thresholds in maternal rats can be blocked by the administration of an opioid antagonist. Premenstrual Syndrome (PMS) has also been investigated in relation to pain response, given that if normal variation in pain response is found across the menstrual cycle as a result of, say, hormonal differences, individuals with PMS will exhibit enhanced differences. Kuczmierczyk *et al.* (1986) report no differences between PMS and non-PMS groups on behavioural measures of pain threshold but significant differences on measures of pain tolerance. It should be noted, however, that consensus is by no means available on the diagnosis of PMS, so that the validity of the group selection criteria is questionable in this study, and further that the abdominal pain frequently associated with PMS may sensitize these individuals to pain.

The examples of internal factors so far relate to a normal population. It is also worth noting, however, that psychiatric populations present a further range of factors. Levels of pain threshold and tolerance are increased in patients with affective illness (e.g. depression) compared to normal controls, with the effects being strongest in male subjects (Davis *et al*. 1979). Results from populations such as these are difficult to interpret because of the well-established biases in attention and concentration associated with anxiety and depression, although Davis and his colleagues report no differences on measures of just noticeable differences. Again there is some evidence for an endogenous opioid mediated mechanism, with Almay and associates reporting a relationship between cerebrospinal fluid opioid binding activity and depth of depressive symptomatology (Davis *et al*. 1979). This presents a strong example of the potential relationships between physiological and psychological mechanisms underlying differences in pain response. Indeed, physical exercise is now used as a treatment for mild to moderate depression, so that the broader implications of endogenous opioid activity has a role in treatments other than simply pain control.

Exogenous factors, rather than simply the endogenous characteristics of individuals, have also been shown to modulate pain response in a controlled laboratory setting. Subjects who publicly described the pain induced previously were subsequently shown to have reduced pain thresholds on later stimulation when compared to those who did not describe their previous pain; tolerance levels were also significantly lower (Jaremko *et al*. 1983). A possible mechanism for this is social learning, whereby the subject learns to express sensation as painful because of previous encouragement to do so. This may be related to clinical findings that information given to pre-surgical patients regarding post-operative pain reduces pain report and analgesia requirement post-operatively, largely through the reduction of anxiety (Egbert *et al*. 1964). Possible support for this comes from evidence that pain stimulates negative self-thoughts (Osman *et al*. 1993), which in turn elevates anxiety and distress. Information presented pre-operatively may serve to break this negative cycle. While the effect appears to be in the opposite direction, the influence of anxiety, and the exacerbation of this following public description of the painful experience, may be operating in a similar way. Information given pre-operatively may serve to reduce anxiety, while public repetition of the painful event may heighten anxiety. Alternatively, the suggestion made by the authors is that this phenomenon lends support to the notion that pain detection and tolerance is mediated to a great extent by the learning of appropriate responses to stimulation, so that there is great scope for individual and cultural differences in pain report, and this can be modified over a short time. That there are two possible explanations does not, however, mean that one has to be wrong, but rather that both might afford a more complete understanding of the phenomenon in question.

Other examples of external factors which mediate response to noxious stimulation include the effects of cigarette smoking. Sult and Moss (1986) report an array of apparently discrepant results, with some studies showing cigarette smoking to be related to increased pain threshold and increased pain tolerance if smoking takes place at the same time as the pain task, and other studies showing no apparent differences between smokers and non-smokers. Indeed the authors themselves were not able to find any significant differences between smokers and non-smokers on either of two pain tasks. The authors explain this discrepancy as being the result of individual differences in the relative strength of nicotine dose resulting from smoking a single cigarette, in particular across smokers and non-smokers. This again illustrates the difficulties associated with any attempt to clearly delineate the factors which mediate pain response. What is clear is that both internal and external factors are of importance, and the mechanisms underlying these may be primarily physiological or primarily psychological or behavioural. It is most likely, however, that both mechanisms are equally valid as potential explanations depending on the specifics of the question being asked. The example of cigarette smoking is a good one because it offers the scope for pharmacological and psychological explanations to be of equal importance, perhaps as a function of individual differences.

Laboratory pain and practical application

At approximately the same time as Melzack and Wall were developing the gate control theory of pain, others were becoming increasingly interested in the psychosocial determinants of pain sensation, with Beecher (1959) being one of the most influential. His criticism of laboratory methods for assessing the function of analgesic assays was therefore largely responsible for the decline in laboratory studies of human pain, although somewhat paradoxically animal studies continued to be presented as good methods for such evaluations. The criticism focused mainly on the inappropriate nature of the laboratory environment, given the range of environmental factors mediating pain information transmission, emphasized by his explanation of lack of pain report in wounded soldiers as being due to the meaning ascribed to the injury. Of course, the laboratory method does not necessarily deny this but instead attempts to hold these factors constant while systematically varying others. Gradually opposition declined as it became clear that laboratory methods could provide valuable supplemental evidence which could contribute to a greater understanding of pain in an ecological setting.

One example is the role that laboratory investigation has played in the development of pain control techniques, such as transcutaneous electrical nerve stimulation (TENS), where mild electrical stimulation is applied to peripheral nerves to achieve pain relief (Price et al. 1994). TENS has been shown to alleviate laboratory induced pain (Garrison and Foreman 1994), and elevate pain threshold and pain tolerance levels, and these results have been replicated in clinical settings (Wolff 1977). Indeed, there is some evidence that the mechanism subsuming the efficacy of TENS as a treatment is the same as that for acupuncture, in particular that C-fibre activity is optimally inhibited by the conjunction of A-beta and A-delta activity (such as would be expected from both TENS and acupuncture treatment) (Lewith and Kenyon 1984). A certain amount of research has been generated regarding the clinical efficacy of acupuncture, and this is now established as a powerful treatment method, primarily for the control of chronic pain (Lewith and Kenyon 1984). It is perhaps revealing that certain psychophysical studies failed to demonstrate a reduction in pain threshold or tolerance following acupuncture in normal subjects (Wolff 1977). Rather than this being damaging evidence, it may instead emphasize the active nature of pain mechanisms, so that acupuncture analgesia may offer pain relief, rather than any prophylactic benefit.

It has already been mentioned that anxiety is often proposed as a factor which predisposes individuals to elevated pain sensation. To an extent this is related to muscle tension as a predisposing factor for pain sensation, and a number of pain-relief strategies rely on the reduction of this tension. This is of particular relevance to childbirth, where there are good reasons for supposing that muscle tension is undesirable and where the use of analgesics is to an extent proscribed. To this end protocols have been developed which attempt to simulate labour pain in the laboratory and thereby establish the efficacy of relaxation techniques during labour. For example, Geden *et al.* (1989) report no benefits of music as a method of reducing muscle tension during analogued labour pain (using finger pressure), although self-guided imagery was found to be beneficial. One weakness of research of this type is the validity of the pain induction method. In the Geden *et al.* study the finger pressure used to induce pain, with the intention of generalizing results to labour pain, clearly has limitations to its ecological validity – again, the cognitive and emotional impact of finger pressure pain will be very different from labour pain. An alternative approach is to assess the effects of previous childbirth experience of pain response in a laboratory environment: Hapidou and DeCatanzaro (1992) report that previous childbirth experience alone is sufficient to elevate pain threshold ratings to experimentally induced pain. As the authors state, 'nothing compares to labor pain' (p. 177), so that the role of past experience and social learning may mediate response to pain experienced both following minor injury and in the laboratory.

Other methods of relaxation, however, have been shown to positively influence levels of pain threshold and tolerance in experimental studies (Jaremko 1978; Beers and Karoly 1979; Berntzen 1987). Linton and Gotestam (1983) report that applied relaxation techniques (where subjects are taught relaxation skills as part of more general coping skills training) are of benefit in coping with painful stimulation (as measured by indices of threshold and tolerance), although advance warning and pre-relaxation was not shown to be of benefit over relaxation after the onset of painful stimulation. Cognitive, as well as behavioural, strategies have been employed in this context: Jaremko (1978) reports improvements in pain tolerance when reversal of affect or rationalization strategies are employed; Hackett and Horan (1980) report that relaxation training results in increased pain tolerance, while distraction and imagery training is related to increased pain threshold. This is again related to the work described above on the coping strategies used spontaneously by athletes, and the degree to which these can be improved by training, although it is probable that distraction is used to elevate tolerance as well as threshold in these cases. There is also evidence (Berntzen *et al.* 1985) that cognitive manipulations can influence the efficacy of analgesic medication. The effects of information given to surgical patients in reducing medication requirements have been briefly described and will be discussed in more detail later. Berntzen and colleagues, however, provide evidence that information can be superior to analgesic medication in reducing pain sensation in laboratory-induced pain. This may be particularly important where the cause of the pain is seen (as in most laboratory studies) and expectancy effects are likely to be important. Berntzen (1987) also presents subsequent evidence that multiple coping strategies (for example, pleasant imagery and distraction) are not significantly more effective than a single strategy. As will be seen subsequently, however, there is evidence that specific strategies are best suited to different individuals. The extent to which these benefits represent potentially effective clinical interventions is significant, and this is evidenced by laboratory studies of tolerance and threshold levels. These include (Rollman 1992):

◆ *inattention* ignoring the pain, frequently by imagining a pain-incompatible situation
◆ *renaming* interpreting the sensation as something other than pain
◆ *distraction* diversion of attention to other mental activities
◆ *somatization* regarding the noxious stimulation as a detached physical event.

While each method is effective independently, optimal pain relief is gained from a conjunction of methods, with techniques varying in effectiveness across individuals. The extent to which these strategies selectively influence the affective and sensory components of pain remains unclear, with effects on verbal report being a further confounding factor. Nevertheless, the efficacy of these techniques, established in laboratory environments and replicated elsewhere, is now accepted.

The cognitive dimension mediating pain response is further highlighted by studies on the effects of mood induction on pain tolerance: Zelman *et al.* (1991) report that depressive mood induction is followed by a reduction in pain tolerance. The extent to which this is related to findings in clinical populations (see pp. 54–7) is unclear, but these results present some intriguing possibilities which are beyond the scope of the current section and will be examined in more detail on pp. 52–7. The notion of a pain-prone personality, for example, may be of more use if the subcharacteristics of this personality dimension, such as depressed mood, are regarded as of primary importance in mediating pain response. Related findings are presented by Dougher *et al.* (1987), who suggest that anxiety enhances pain responsivity, but only if the source of the anxiety is related to the painful stimulus. The relationship between anxiety and depression is well established, although in this instance there are likely to be further mediating factors such as the nature of the painful stimulus.

One final intervention method designed to elevate pain threshold and tolerance is hypnotic suggestion, which has enjoyed a certain vogue recently. Dahlgren *et al.* (1995) report that hypnotic induction and analgesia suggestion reduces pain intensity report, while hypnotic induction and relaxation suggestion reduces pain unpleasantness report. This apparent dissociation of the sensory and affective components of pain is consistent with the multidimensional nature of pain proposed here, with each seemingly capable of being influenced independently. Furthermore, Price and Barber (1987) present evidence that hypnotic suggestion which is not specific in this way reduces pain report on both sensory and affective dimensions, which implies a certain interaction between the two, so that any independence is not absolute. This is supported by Kiernan *et al.* (1995), who emphasize the role of multiple mechanisms of pain reduction by hypnotic suggestion. Interestingly, Price and Barber (1987) also report that this interactive effect is greatest for relatively high levels of painful stimulation and weakest for near-threshold painful stimulation. The reasons for this are unclear. Although Price and Barber use indirect hypnotic suggestion and Dahlgren *et al.* (1995) use direct suggestion, evidence from Lynn *et al.* (1993) suggests that the two methods produce similar results and are therefore comparable.

Studies like these are clearly of value in demonstrating the efficacy, validity and mechanism of interventions designed to modulate pain response in a clinical environment. Indeed, some surgeons are now employing hypnotic suggestion as the pain control method of choice for certain procedures. The advantages of this approach are clear, namely that large subject groups can be employed without the difficulties attending research in a clinical environment, and the risk of disrupting the normal function of clinical staff. Perhaps more importantly, research of this kind presents clear avenues for further research in an ecological setting, so that the validity of findings can be further tested. While it is useful to begin research into, for example, cognitive pain control strategies in a laboratory environment, ultimately the efficacy of these must be tested on patient groups.

Both the limitations and advantages of laboratory studies are clear; however, the majority of the limitations stem from a conceptual understanding of the nature of pain which is now grossly outmoded. If this is properly understood there is potential for laboratory studies to continue to be valuable sources of evidence regarding the nature of pain mechanisms. What is important to realize is that only certain classes of questions can be answered by investigations of this sort, so that attempts to equate laboratory pain with clinical pain must proceed with caution. Evidence for the role of psychological factors is now accepted, and it is situations such as these where these factors will be of utmost importance. Given the active and interactive nature of pain mechanisms, it is perhaps unreasonable to hope that it will be possible to hold these constant across individuals. This suggests that for genuine advances to be made, particularly in the application of theory to practice, laboratory studies must proceed alongside studies carried out in a naturalistic setting.

Conclusion

Laboratory studies on pain derive from two distinct research agendas: the physiological, with attempts to delineate the degree of specificity in the peripheral nervous system, and the mechanism by which this impacts on the higher, central nervous system; and the psychophysical, with attempts to relate phenomena and stimuli in the physical world to experiental phenomena. The latter provides the role model for much of this research, focusing on such aspects of pain response as threshold and tolerance, i.e. the sensory parameters of pain. More recently, such studies have extended their range of interests to incorporate psychological moderators of pain response (as well as physical), so that anxiety and hypnotic suggestion, for example, have been investigated in laboratory environments. Studies in the laboratory have all the advantages of investigation under controlled conditions, and all the disadvantages of attempting to model a dynamic, complex system with reference only to the stimulus-response features of this system. It is arguable that the historical influence of psychophysics, particularly its initial interest with perceptual senses such as vision, has distorted the understanding of the role of pain as a need state rather than a perceptual process.

References

Albe-Fessard, D. and Fessard, A. (1975) Recent advances on the neurophysiological bases of pain sensation. *Acta Neurobiologiae Experimentalis*, 35: 715–40.

Apkarian, A.V., Stea, R.A. and Bolanowski, S.J. (1994) Heat-induced pain dimishes vibrotactile perception: a touch gate. *Somatosensory and Motor Research*, 11: 259–67.

Beecher, H.K. (1959) *Measurement of Subjective Responses*. New York: Oxford University Press.

Beers, T.M. and Karoly, P. (1979) Cognitive strategies, expectancy, and coping style in the control of pain. *Journal of Consulting and Clinical Psychology*, 47: 179–80.

Berntzen, D. (1987) Effects of multiple cognitive coping strategies on laboratory pain. *Cognitive Therapy and Research*, 11: 613–23.

Berntzen, D., Fors, E. and Gotestam, K.G. (1985) Effects of an analgesic drug (paralgin forte) upon laboratory pain under different cognitive manipulations: an experimental study. *Acta Neurologica Scandinavica*, 72: 30–5.

Croze, S. and Duclaux, R. (1978) Subordination of intolerance to threshold in thermal pain. *Brain Research*, 154: 214–17.

Cubelli, R., Caselli, M. and Neri, M. (1984) Pain endurance in unilateral cerebral lesions. *Cortex*, 20: 369–75.

Dahlgren, L.A., Kurtz, R.M., Strube, M.J. and Malone, M.D. (1995) Differential effects of hypnotic suggestion on multiple dimensions of pain. *Journal of Pain and Symptom Management*, 10: 464–70.

Davis, G.C., Buchsbaum, M.S. and Bunney, W.E. (1979) Analgesia to painful stimuli in affective illness. *American Journal of Psychiatry*, 136: 1148–51.

Dougher, M.J., Goldstein, D. and Leight, K.A. (1987) Induced anxiety and pain. *Journal of Anxiety Disorders*, 1: 259–64.

Egbert, L.D., Battit, M.D., Welch, C.E. and Bartlett, M.K. (1964) Reduction of postoperative pain by encouragement and instruction of patients. *New England Journal of Medicine*, 270: 825–7.

Garrison, D.W. and Foreman, R.D. (1994) Decreased activity of spontaneous and noxiously evoked dorsal horn cells during transcutaneous electrical nerve stimulation (TENS). *Pain*, 58: 309–15.

Geden, E.A., Lower, M., Beattie, S. and Beck, N.S. (1989) Effects of music and imagery on physiologic and self-report of analogued labor pain. *Nursing Research*, 38: 37–41.

Goolkasian, P. (1985) Phase and sex effects in pain experience: a critical review. *Psychology of Women Quarterly*, 9: 15–28.

Hackett, G. and Horan, J.J. (1980) Stress inoculation for pain: what's really going on? *Journal of Counselling Psychology*, 27: 107–16.

Hapidou, E.G. and DeCatanzaro, D. (1992) Responsiveness to laboratory pain in women as a function of age and childbirth pain experience. *Pain*, 48: 177–81.

Jamner, L.D. and Schwartz, G.E. (1986) Self-deception predicts self-report and endurance of pain. *Psychosomatic Medicine*, 48: 211–23.

Janal, M.N., Glusman, M., Kuhl, J.P. and Clark, W.C. (1994) On the absence of correlation between responses to noxious heat, cold, electrical and ischemic stimulation. *Pain*, 58: 403–11.

Jaremko, M.E. (1978) Cognitive strategies in the control of pain tolerance. *Journal of Behavior Therapy and Experimental Psychiatry*, 9: 239–44.

Jaremko, M.E., Silbert, L. and Mann, T. (1981) The differential ability of athletes and nonathletes to cope with two types of pain: a radical behavioral model. *Psychological Record*, 31: 265–75.

Jaremko, M.E., Crusko, A.H. and Lau, G. (1983) Effects of public description on the detection and tolerance of pain. *Journal of Behavior Therapy and Experimental Psychiatry*, 14: 43–8.

Kiernan, B.D., Dane, J.R., Phillips, L.H. and Price, D.D. (1995) Hypnotic analgesia reduces R-III nociceptive reflex: farther evidence concerning the multifactorial nature of hypnotic analgesia. *Pain*, 60: 39–47.

Kuczmierczyk, A.R., Adams, H.E., Calhoun, K.S. and Naor, S. (1986) Pain responsivity in women with premenstrual syndrome across the menstrual cycle. *Perceptual and Motor Skills*, 63: 387–93.

Lewith, G.T. and Kenyon, J.N. (1984) Physiological and psychological explanations for the mechanism of acupuncture as a treatment for chronic pain. *Social Science and Medicine*, 19: 1367–78.

Linton, S.J. and Gotestam, K.G. (1983) Applied relaxation (coping) in control of laboratory pain: effects of signalled pain and instructions of when to relax. *Psychological Reports*, 53: 467–76.

Lynn, S.J., Neufeld, V. and Mare, C. (1993) Direct versus indirect suggestions: a conceptual and methodological review. *International Journal of Clinical and Experimental Hypnosis*, 41: 124–52.

Neri, M., Vecchi, G.P. and Caselli, M. (1985) Pain measurement in right–left cerebral lesions. *Neuropsychologia*, 23: 123–6.

Neufeld, R.W. and Thomas, P. (1977) Effects of perceived efficacy of a prophylactic controlling mechanism on self-control under pain stimulation. *Canadian Journal of Behavioural Science*, 9: 224–32.

Osman, A., Bunger, S., Osman, J.R. and Fisher, L. (1993) The inventory of negative thoughts in response to pain: factor structure and psychometric properties in a college sample. *Journal of Behavioral Medicine*, 16: 219–24.

Price, D.D. and Barber, J. (1987) An analysis of factors that contribute to the efficacy of hypnotic analgesia. *Journal of Abnormal Psychology*, 96: 46–51.

Price, D.D., Rafii, A., Watkins, L.R. and Buckingham, B. (1994) A psychophysical analysis of acupuncture analgesia. *Pain*, 19: 27–42.

Rollman, G.B. (1992) Cognitive effects in pain and pain judgements, in D. Algom (ed.) *Psychophysical Approaches to Cognition*. Amsterdam: North Holland.

Sult, S.C. and Moss, R.A. (1986) The effects of cigarette smoking on the perception of electrical stimulation and cold pressor pain. *Addictive Behaviors*, 11: 447–51.

Wall, P.D. (1979) On the relation of pain to injury. *Pain*, 6: 253–64.

Wall, P.D. (1983) Pain as a need state. *Journal of Psychosomatic Research*, 27: 413.

Wolff, B.B. (1977) The role of laboratory pain induction methods in the systematic study of human pain. *Acupuncture and Electro Therapeutics Research*, 2: 271–305.

Zelman, D.C, Howland, E.W., Nichols, S.N. and Cleeland, C.S. (1991) The effects of induced mood on laboratory pain. *Pain*, 46: 105–11.

Acute and chronic dimensions

Felix qui potuit rerum cognoscere causas.
Fortunate is he who has been able to understand the causes of things.

(Virgil, *Georgics*)

Summary

Psychological, social and behavioural factors impact on and mediate pain responses at all stages, whether the pain is acute or chronic and regardless of the cause. The specifics of these factors are discussed, with particular reference to ecological studies on pain patients, and the extent to which these relate to experimental findings. That these factors exist does not mean, however, that they are of constant importance; the suggestion is made that the relative importance of different factors varies over time. Immediately after injury physiological mechanisms are largely responsible for the mediation of pain response; as this pain continues, however, psychological, social and behavioural factors increase in importance, and continue to do so as the pain persists. This provides indications of how chronic and persistent pain patients develop the behavioural and cognitive characteristics which typify their condition.

Introduction

The study of pain has been beset with problems of definition throughout its history, being variously described in physiological, somatic, cognitive, affective and cultural terms. The International Association for the Study of Pain (cited in Craig 1984: 835) defines pain as 'An unpleasant sensory and emotional experience associated with actual or potential tissue damage, or described in terms of such damage'. This tacitly acknowledges the role that personal meaning and subjective experience plays (Wall 1983), but at the same time the definition becomes largely meaningless by attempting to incorporate all possible facets of pain without sufficient analysis. A flexible and indistinct definition is, in this case, no definition at all; it is unlikely that any single definition of pain will be comprehensive and satisfy all: while some focus on the affective components of pain, others on the sensory, and still others on the physiological, these are all simply different perspectives from which to assess the problem. The problem of definition has already become apparent, given that each study incorporates implicit assumptions about the nature of the phenomena under study; this is not necessarily a bad thing, given that instead of attempting to formulate a unifying definition of pain one should instead present the definition from which one is working and then proceed. Much of the confusion is the result of a failure to state explicitly what question is being asked, and from what perspective an answer will be sought. Moreover, as one moves away from studies at the level of physiological mechanism and begins to investigate psychosocial and behavioural variables this problem becomes exacerbated by the very variables under investigation, given, for example, the extent to which psychological and behavioural variables overlap and interact.

What is perhaps most important about the IASP definition given above is that it refers to the role of 'actual or *potential* tissue damage' (emphasis added), and it is perhaps this which presents one feature which ties together all aspects of pain: pain is defined with reference to tissue damage, as this is the usual, 'normal', and paradigmatic case. Nevertheless, this is neither necessary nor sufficient for pain to exist, a contention made earlier, and as such can be used as a common point of reference only when discussing more complex aspects of pain. This is related to the somewhat philosophical question of how pain becomes defined in a linguistic and cultural context, where pain expression (both verbal and behavioural) is to an extent learned (for a more detailed analysis see Hilbert 1984).

A common area of confusion is between acute and chronic dimensions of pain, which may be in part the consequence of a cultural understanding of pain as a transient phenomenon, so that attempts to provide a model for pain mechanisms proceed with acute pain as the paradigm example. It is here that the unifying feature of pain, as defined *in the first instance* by acute tissue damage, can lead to confusion and a misunderstanding of the nature of the situation. Chronic pain is subsequently defined as acute pain which remains unresolved; however, chronic pain is not simply the conjunction of pain and chronicity (or persistence), although many view it as such. Indeed a clinical diagnosis of chronic pain may simply require the continuance of pain over a pre-specified interval, but chronic pain, as referred to herein, is not the same as persistent pain. This traditional conception of chronic pain as being definable by duration is misleading, and furthermore the distinction between acute and chronic dimensions of pain is not as clear as is often assumed. There are numerous cases of pain persisting over time where the characteristics usual in chronic pain patients do not exist or exist in a modified fashion (e.g. cancer pain, rheumatoid arthritis), and other cases of intermitting, acute episodes of pain which continue over time but are not persistent (e.g. burns pain, migraine headache). As will be seen, the nature of chronic pain allows for the development of psychological, social and behavioural factors which are of far less importance in acute cases. The extent to which chronic pain (as a pathological condition) is related to persistent pain and intermittent acute pain presents another dimension to this.

With some notable exceptions, laboratory studies such as those detailed in the previous chapter investigate acute pain, largely due to the nature of the stimuli used, but also because of the common acceptance of this as the normal manifestation of pain. The confusion here lies in equating the paradigm case defining pain with an expectation of what model pain phenomena should conform to. Physiological and psychological studies both tend to be more representative of the spectrum of pain dimensions, but there is nevertheless an implicit assumption that acute pain is the exemplar case, with chronic pain being a pathological extension of this, with the only difference being duration. There is substantial evidence, however, that chronic pain is quite different in its nature, at all levels of explanation, from acute pain, although at the same time it is misguided to regard the two phenomena as fundamentally distinct. This apparent paradox will, it is hoped, be resolved later in this book; it will suffice to say now that the difference lies in the potential for certain influences to be expressed as pain persists over time, a potential which does not exist in acute cases, and as such there must be an account of the continuum from acute to chronic pain, with reference to cases where this transition does not occur.

From a clinical perspective the matter is perhaps more simple, in that with a few important exceptions it is clear whether pain relief is directed at a patient suffering from acute pain or chronic pain. Post-operative or trauma pain, for example, is a clear case of acute pain, while low back pain which has remained unresolved for several years is a clear case of chronic pain. Other cases, which do not fall neatly into this description of acute and chronic pain as poles on a continuum include burns pain, cancer pain, rheumatoid arthritis pain, among others. This suggests that while the notion of a continuum might represent a convenient shorthand (in the same way that the notion of a gate is a useful metaphor), this simply offers a method for understanding the various psychological, social and behavioural factors at work which, in other cases, may act quite differently. There is a substantial literature, albeit a fragmented one, which outlines the psychosocial and behavioural variables that mediate the individual's response in these situations, and which complements existing physiological and psychophysical results, so that gradually we begin to arrive at a more holistic understanding of pain. It is the distinction between acute and chronic dimensions of pain, which in the past has been the source of confusion and misguided research, that perhaps presents the key to any integration of different research avenues.

Acute pain

In any discussion of differences and similarities across acute and chronic dimensions of pain, there is perhaps a greater range of issues in acute pain. While generally being regarded as the 'normal' manifestation of some physical pathology, the range of syndromes and diseases where there is pain that resolves (i.e. is acute) is vast, in contrast to the relatively narrow range of situations where pain does not resolve. If we are to begin with the assumption that acute pain and chronic pain can usefully be regarded as at ends of a spectrum, rather than fundamentally separate conditions, it is reasonable to begin with the most common manifestation of this. Indeed, for both the patient, concerned with personal well-being, and the physician, seeking a diagnosis, pain represents the single most important symptom indicating that something is amiss. It has been reported as being the primary symptom in 80 per cent of presentations (Turk 1994), emphasizing its salience for the patient at least. The value of pain as a diagnostic tool is unchallenged; however, it is too common for pain to be regarded as only and always reflecting some underlying physical pathology. While this is true in most cases (and even if physical pathology cannot be detected this does not necessarily imply it does not exist) it is important to be aware that in some cases psychological, social and behavioural factors may be of greater importance and relevance in the diagnosis and treatment of the patient than, say, tissue damage.

What is of central importance in the current discussion, however, does not depend solely on this diversity. It is equally important to emphasize that similar levels of dysfunction and physical pathology, for example in trauma patients, can result in very different levels of pain across patients. One individual may require no pain medication, whereas pain control may never be achieved in another. Clearly there is not a linear relationship between the nature of the cause of the pain and the pain itself, and this fact remains whether one is discussing post-operative pain, headache pain, or any other type of pain. The factors which mediate this response have been most comprehensively investigated in two settings: laboratory studies and post-operative pain. While the former has been discussed previously, the latter will provide the basis of the current discussion; one compelling reason for this is that surgical pain presents an ecologically valid situation while giving the researcher the opportunity to systematically control certain variables.

The extent to which pain control and the prediction of pain in surgical patients is of importance in the clinical setting is emphasized by Puntillo and Weiss (1994). Taking critically ill cardiovascular patients, Puntillo and Weiss report that subjects with higher levels of pain intensity also had significantly elevated levels of post-operative complication (atelectasis, in this case). Although this was the only post-operative complication to be related to pain intensity in this study, this may be due to the low incidence of other complications, so that these effects may have been of insufficient power to produce a detectable effect. This is further supported by a review of similar literature which has shown a relationship between levels of pain intensity and analgesic practice, and post-operative outcome and incidence of complication (Puntillo and Weiss 1994). Research of this sort, taken as a whole, indicates that pain is not simply a distressing symptom but also a significant predictor of complication and outcome, so that inadequate pain control can be the precursor of poor morbidity and increased mortality. To this end, research attempting to delineate the predictors of pain in surgical patients, and the extent to which the efficacy of pain control methods can be enhanced by targeting specific resources at those individuals most likely to benefit is of paramount importance in clinical practice. This is in addition to the clear theoretical value of investigating the role of, for example, self-efficacy beliefs, in mediating pain response in an ecological setting as opposed to a laboratory environment and providing a test-bed for the generalization of results established experimentally.

As a result of the theoretical and clinical application of such results, the literature investigating the relationship between pre-operative and post-operative predictors of pain following surgery is vast, and only a (we hope) representative sample can be described here. Of the variables investigated, anxiety is perhaps the most common, and it is now relatively well established that pre-operative anxiety predicts post-operative anxiety and distress, measured psychometrically, behaviourally or physiologically. Anxiety may be measured using self-report questionnaires, by rating patients independently on the basis of verbal and physical behaviour, or by measuring heart rate, blood pressure, and so on. These measures tend to correlate highly and all predict post-operative anxiety and distress. The relationship between anxiety and pain, however, is unclear, and the evidence remains equivocal. Martinez-Urrutia (1975) reports a positive and significant correlation between state anxiety (as measured using the State-Trait Anxiety Inventory) and post-operative pain, and these findings have been replicated elsewhere. Unfortunately negative results have also been reported, and this is perhaps not surprising given the wealth of confounding factors which exist in a clinical environment, not least the desire by ward staff to provide adequate pain control, thereby reducing variance in individual pain response necessary for the detection of weak effects. There is, however, a stronger, more coherent body of evidence that post-operative outcome can to some extent be predicted by pre-operative psychosocial, behavioural and physiological variables, although exactly which factors can be predicted remains unclear. Given an operational definition of outcome following surgery, certain factors will predict variance in this. A definitive list of variables cannot be given, however, as these will depend to a great extent on the definition of outcome used. Wolfer and Davis (1970) highlight many of the difficulties associated with research of this type, in particular the variety of post-operative factors which it is possible, at least potentially, to assess, and provide a fairly comprehensive definition in their own investigation. This includes psychological, behavioural and physical measures, with both patient and nurse ratings being included. The history of this research continues so that Taenzer *et al.* (1986) still wrestle with the same problem of incomparable results across studies, largely as a result of this difficulty in arriving at a common definition of outcome. They report that approximately half the variance in post-operative outcome could be predicted by a battery of pre-operative test variables which included anxiety, extraversion, depression, past experience of chronic pain and medication-use bias. This study defined outcome with reference to self-reported pain and distress (anxiety and depression), which addresses only the psychological state of the patient, and then only a part of this. Variance in the type of surgery performed and different treatment methods across countries and even within them present other difficulties in generalizing results and drawing comparisons, a dilemma for which there is unfortunately no clear solution.

Theory and clinical practice in acute pain

Research of this nature can be traced to a seminal piece of work by Egbert *et al.* (1964), who compared the recovery and analgesia intake of patients who had been given encouragement and information pre-operatively to those who had not received such special treatment. The results were striking: the special care group rated themselves as more comfortable, were rated as in better physical and emotional condition, requested fewer analgesics, and were discharged earlier. The study conflated behavioural and cognitive interventions, but showed clearly that patient outcome could be influenced by factors other than the physical pathology or direct physical treatment. This stimulated the gradual nascence of research into the psychological, social and behavioural factors of importance in acute, clinical pain, including inpatient surgery (e.g. Cohen and Lazarus 1973) and outpatient surgery (e.g. Jamison *et al.* 1987). As described above, the most commonly investigated pre-operative factors include various measures of anxiety and distress: these include depression (Taenzer *et al.* 1986), fear of surgery (Martinez-Urrutia 1975), trait anxiety (Wallace 1987), and a variety of physiological indices (Wolfer and Davis 1970) such as heart rate, palmar sweat index and catecholamine secretion. Unfortunately there is a risk of confounding state effects with trait effects when one investigates mood, so that a given individual may report more distress because of elevated state anxiety or may report both more distress and elevated state anxiety because of an underlying anxious disposition. There is significant overlap here with the effects of personality and coping styles: Taenzer *et al.* (1986) suggest that certain individuals may be predisposed to using medication (indeed, the reverse may also be true – see pp. 80–3); this may be due to a physiological sensitivity to opioids, for example, or the result of a social learning process.

Related to any exegesis of the role of personality (however defined) is the notion of coping: it is possible that the personality factors which have been identified as relevant to the mediation of pain responses may in fact simply reflect the consistent adoption of a given coping or cognitive style. This may be dispositional, or a style adopted at the time of threat (Cohen and Lazarus 1973). Certain such styles may be adaptive in a surgical environment: Janis (1958) has suggested that there exists a subgroup of individuals who utilize denial to the extent of exhibiting very low, maladaptive levels of anxiety, so that there is a curvilinear relationship between pre-operative anxiety and outcome, with a moderate level of anxiety being optimal. Support for this, however, has not been demonstrated (Johnston and Carpenter 1980; Wallace 1986). Rather than being maladaptive, avoidant strategies may instead improve the recovery of the patient, if this facilitates a reduction in anxiety (Suls and Fletcher 1985). Information presentation, while at first glance inconsistent with this, may act in a similar way: that is, the reduction of anxiety. The short-term and long-term consequences of different strategies are areas of interest (Suls and Fletcher 1985): denial may be maximally effective in the short term but maladaptive if the pain fails to resolve over time.

An alternative strategy is one where control is sought, which may be regarded as one non-avoidant strategy (unlike denial). This has commonly been exemplified by information-giving, although behavioural control is possible (see patient controlled analgesia, pp. 56–7). Certainly information has been found to improve adjustment and recovery, as well as pain tolerance in experimental pain (Staub and Kellett 1972; Klos *et al.* 1980). However, it has been suggested that the provision of information to patients exhibiting denial strategies may worsen outcome (Wilson 1981; Smith *et al.* 1984). It is clear that the varied conceptions of coping and personality overlap, with denial, non-avoidance, information-seeking, desire for control and active coping being some of the descriptors of varied patient responses; however, these are not exclusive categories. Furthermore, it should not be assumed that one strategy is best for all patients, or that each strategy acts independently (Jensen *et al.* 1991; Krohne *et al.* 1996).

Jensen *et al.* (1991) suggest that social learning theory may provide us with a model of the factors influencing coping efforts, including self-efficacy beliefs, outcome expectancies and past experience. The different individual variables mediating pain response will be outlined in more detail in subsequent sections. The point being made here is that the diverse range of factors influencing recovery from surgery, in particular pain response (including subjective report, behaviour, analgesia requirement, and so on), represent those factors which have to be incorporated in any adequate and comprehensive model of acute pain. These may not represent the only factors which mediate pain response, but they are certainly important given the ecological validity of the setting in which they have been shown to act.

It is notable that for all of the effort expended attempting to predict post-operative recovery, there is also a notable lack of proposed mechanisms by which pre-operative anxiety, say, might influence post-operative pain. A relatively simple explanation might be that pre-operative anxiety predicts post-operative anxiety (a fairly well-established finding), and that this post-operative anxiety results in muscle tension and subsequently elevated levels of pain. Even explanations as simple and intuitive as these, however, are lacking in many studies, which perhaps illustrates the different research agenda of academics and clinicians working in apparently the same field. Certainly there is a tendency for studies to be largely descriptive. While establishing a relationship between a pre-operative variable and post-operative outcome may present avenues for the development of interventions to proceed along, it is insufficient to simply state that 'descending factors', as described by Melzack and Wall (1982), offer a possible explanation for this effect. Not least this is lacking because hypotheses are rarely presented which can be tested and thereby supported or disproved.

One illustration of the ways in which academic and clinical findings can complement each other is given by the rapid and extensive adoption of patient controlled analgesia (PCA) in post-operative environments, where patients are given the ability to administer their own doses of, say, morphine. While there are constraints on what the patient can administer for safety reasons, the central feature of devices such as these is that they present patients with an opportunity to control, albeit to a limited extent, their own environment. This is related to more theoretical findings that self-efficacy beliefs are related to post-operative outcome, with low efficacy beliefs being associated with poor outcome. The benefits of PCA may stem in part from the facilitation of self-efficacy beliefs, as well as the clear advantages of relatively immediate, predictable pain relief and the ability to bypass patients' reluctance to request medication. These individual differences in coping strategies are discussed in greater detail in subsequent sections, but are of primary importance in surgical settings. Patients given this element of control over their environment show significant differences in pain levels and medication requirements when compared to those given nurse administered or continuous infusion pain medication, reporting less pain and using less medication (Lehmann *et al.* 1990). Reductions in post-operative inpatient stay have also been reported in PCA patients (Thomas *et al.* 1993), so that there is evidence for a benefit on both psychological and behavioural measures. While the exact mechanism underlying this remains unclear, it provides an example of the strength of psychological factors (such as the self-efficacy beliefs) in the mediation of pain; furthermore, this is an encouraging example of the use to which such theoretical findings may be applied to the benefit of clinicians. Finally, the theoretical importance of such findings is that they can be comfortably accommodated by gate control theory (and signal detection theory) and validate experimental results from laboratory studies.

While there is overwhelming evidence that PCA is generally effective when the effect on a population is measured, there has recently been an interest in the specific factors which determine those patients most (or least) likely to benefit from the administration of PCA. Thomas and her colleagues (1995) report that patients with high levels of state anxiety experienced the greatest relative improvement in pain control when compared to a control group. Indeed, one problem reported with the use of PCA is the tendency of some patients (possibly an identifiable subgroup) to misuse the PCA pump and treat it as an anxiolytic device, administering morphine when anxiety is felt rather than pain. In certain cases this has resulted in overdose and subsequent respiratory depression (Stuart Taylor, personal communication). Further, Johnson *et al.* (1989) present evidence that patients with an internal locus of control experience the greatest benefit from the use of PCA, while patients with a history of chronic pain benefit less from PCA (Magnani *et al.* 1989). The latter finding is arguably the result of chronic pain patients redefining 'normal' levels of pain, so that what would be described as moderate pain by normal subjects is accommodated by chronic pain sufferers. It is the first finding, that locus of control mediates PCA efficacy, which is most revealing of the mechanism underlying the benefits of PCA. This is perhaps related to the suggestion made by Wilder-Smith and Schuler (1992) that patients' own attitudes towards pain medication mediate the degree to which such medication is permitted. Evidence that education can increase patient uptake of pain medication offered will clearly have concomitant effects on the extent to which such medication is self-administered (Wilder-Smith and Schuler 1992). Some patients exhibit a reluctance to take pain medication, which may be of relevance to the debate concerning the apparent lack of pain following injury (in both soldiers and civilians – see p. 5). Should this be regarded as a confound in attempts to delineate the factors modulating post-operative pain, or as a factor in its own right?

Laboratory studies and studies on surgical populations therefore present complementary lines of research which have led to the identification of several variables central to the mediation of pain response where the cause of the pain is clear. While these two environments do not represent a comprehensive account of situations which result in pain, we at least can make advances in the development of both theoretical models and treatment methods. As this continues, the next question is the extent to which these findings relate to pain which does not resolve over time.

Chronic pain

There is a substantial lack of understanding regarding the development of chronic pain, and subsequent incapacity, in the absence of any discernible physical pathology, disease or neuropathy. This is exacerbated by the scale of the problem itself: Turk (1994) reports that costs exceed $70 billion per annum in the USA. It is, therefore, perhaps not surprising that historically there has been a split between research motivated by a desire to improve patient care, and that motivated by a desire to advance knowledge. While this is true in all medical and related sciences, the distinction is particularly striking in the case of chronic pain.

Advances in the treatment of chronic pain patients have benefited in particular from the incorporation of psychological models, which contrasts with traditional medical approaches to the problem of chronic pain which largely ignore psychological factors. These advances in treatment have closely followed changes in how pain is conceptualized and assessed. Most important of these developments is the acceptance that chronicity alone is insufficient to characterize the chronic pain patient. What characterizes patients with unresolved pain is the chronic pain syndrome, a state of being defined along certain behavioural, affective and cognitive dimensions, with any physical or physiological dimension of pain being neither a necessary nor a sufficient condition for the existence of the syndrome. It is important to regard pain in this case as a symptom rather than a disease; if we are to refer to a disease it should be the chronic pain syndrome that we refer to, with chronic pain itself being the paramount symptom. It soon becomes clear that it is not possible to investigate chronic pain in isolation, as one is dealing with a patient influenced by other, secondary, factors that are too intimately involved to be held constant.

In the past the treatment of the chronic pain patient has relied on a narrow conception of the genesis of the chronic pain syndrome (Novy *et al.* 1995). Pharmacological and surgical treatment are still widely used, but these have several drawbacks and assume some underlying physical pathology, again presuming a pain which is identical in nature and cause to acute pain resulting from tissue damage. As a result, bedrest, medication, crutches and surgery are often the treatments offered (Meilman 1984), and as will be seen these may have a quite negative effect on the patient, serving to reinforce the behaviours which have developed in an attempt to cope with the failure of the pain to resolve. Indeed, there remain physicians who regard patients that do not conform to this model as suffering from pain which is in some sense not 'real', despite overwhelming behavioural evidence to the contrary. A broader conception of pain and its aetiology, however, has led to the introduction of other treatment methods, including cognitive and behavioural interventions, which have produced some striking results. The strength of these is that they do not assume, or rely upon, any physical pathology existing as the cause of the pain. The danger, however, is that the identification of psychological, social and behavioural factors which contribute to the development and maintenance of chronic pain leads to the view that chronic pain is 'a distinctly different entity from acute pain' (Meilman 1984: 307). Instead, these factors will be regarded here as those which may well serve an adaptive purpose in the short term but which increasingly become maladaptive as the pain persists.

It is, then, the very nature of chronic pain, the extension over time, that presents greater scope for psychological, social and behavioural factors to mediate the individual's response to their condition. Specifically, it has been argued persuasively by Fordyce originally and then others that the nature of the chronic pain syndrome presents opportunities for unconscious learning (Fordyce *et al.* 1968). The argument of Fordyce is that certain behaviours typically exhibited by chronic pain syndrome patients appear to be describable with reference to an operant-conditioning model. That is, requests for pain medication, for example, are reinforced by attention from others and the prescription of medication (not least the narcotic effect of the medication itself). Attention and medication, in this case, act as reinforcers to the behaviour of medication request, in the same way that a button which, when pressed, releases food soon leads to the association of the button and the food in animal studies. This behaviourist model then, if the initial premise is accepted, suggests ways in which chronic pain syndrome patients may be treated, with an emphasis being on breaking associations which have been created between behaviours and rewards. Furthermore, it highlights ways in which chronic pain syndrome patients should specifically *not* be treated, because of the potential for the reinforcement of maladaptive behaviours, and these unfortunately correspond with the treatments commonly offered for unresolved pain (i.e. bedrest, medication, surgery). These factors are discussed in more detail in subsequent sections.

Theory and clinical practice in chronic pain

The development of treatment programmes based on this approach have produced some quite remarkable results, although these programmes are not without their critics. Perhaps the strength of this approach, notwithstanding the undeniable benefits which result, is that it entirely bypasses much of the controversy associated with chronic pain; Fordyce is keen to emphasize that pain *per se* is not his concern, but rather the behaviours associated with being in pain and this condition not resolving (Fordyce 1984: 866). 'Pain behaviours may . . . occur in the absence of nociception because they lead to the consequence of avoiding aversive events. That would be an instance of avoidance learning.' While tissue damage, or apparent lack thereof, is assumed by many to be the primary distinguishing factor between acute and chronic pain, certainly by many clinicians, this has led (as mentioned above) to debate concerning at what time pain should be regarded as chronic. Six months is suggested as a figure as this is thought to be sufficient for all tissue healing to take place (Meilman 1984), but this disregards physical pathology which cannot be determined, burns treatment where painful episodes may continue for several months, rheumatoid arthritis and other degenerative conditions, cancer pain, and so on. Furthermore, six months may well be sufficient time for the psychological and behavioural factors identified by Fordyce and others to modify behaviour, so that the entire debate appears to be missing the point of Fordyce's argument. Fordyce avoids this debate, and resulting confusion, by focusing on the rehabilitation of the patient. In extreme cases the chronic pain patient is unable to function independently, often being house-bound and reliant on large quantities of medication. From this perspective, it is the rehabilitation of the patient which becomes of greater importance than the pain itself, given that all efforts which have been made to resolve any physical pathology underlying the pain have met with little or no success.

Fordyce's model turns on the premise that the behaviours typical of the chronic pain patient (inactivity, medication request, medication consumption, etc.) are reinforceable by the environment and other individuals. Behaviours have consequences, and if these consequences can be characterized as favourable, the behaviour eliciting them will tend to be reinforced. These favourable consequences of pain behaviours have been termed gain, and subdivided into primary, secondary and tertiary gain (Bokan *et al.* 1981). The first refers to any interpersonal, psychological mechanism for the reduction of unacceptable affect or conflict, the second to the interpersonal or environmental advantage supplied by the behaviour, and the last to any advantage that someone other than the patient may gain from the behaviour. There is substantial evidence for the effects of the environmental and interpersonal reinforcers: if a supportive spouse is present during a medical interview the patient will rate the pain as higher, whereas with an unsupportive spouse the reverse is the case (Roberts and Reinhardt 1980). Furthermore, the interactions may be quite subtle: Biglan (1991: 157) highlights the fact that many behaviours associated with distress (e.g. pain) are non-verbal, appearing to form 'a functional response class which has a unique impact on others'. The operant reinforcement of these behaviours is not conscious, and any advantage ascribed to such behaviours has to be understood in the context of a patient who believes that the pain will never resolve, and so seeks relief in other ways. Fordyce is not suggesting that pain is produced by operant conditioning, but that pain is attended by certain behaviours, and these behaviours are subject to specific influences, such as operant conditioning, *over time* (Fordyce 1984). The temporal feature of chronic pain is important, then, but not as an indicator of whether tissue healing has occurred. Instead it is a necessary condition for certain behavioural and psychological processes to act.

Treatment of chronic pain behaviours, then, relies on the extinction of associations between specific distressed behaviours and reinforcers, so that patients are no longer given medication on request, for example. Further, an attempt is made to *establish* associations between well behaviours and reinforcers, such as giving strong encouragement to patients who attempt to be self-mobile. In this way, an attempt is made to reverse the development of the behavioural state of the patient and achieve a higher level of function. The result of studies concerning the efficacy of behavioural treatment programmes are striking: Roberts and Reinhardt (1980), for example, report that 77 per cent of treated patients were leading 'normal lives without medication', compared to almost none in the untreated group. Psychological adjustment, as measured on the Minnesota Multiphasic Personality Inventory, was also improved in the treated group. This is in the context of a population previously seriously disabled by their condition and unable to function independently, where traditional medical interventions had failed to provide significant relief. These programmes are not without their critics, however: claims have variously been made that patients are being taught to be stoical, or that the highly selective nature of the programmes means that the results are not generalizable (Turner and Chapman 1982; Turk and Rudy 1990a). A further critique might focus on the narrow description of pain behaviour, which is to an extent proscriptive and ignores possibly *adaptive* behaviours. Fordyce *et al.* (1985) respond by arguing that their principal objective is not to modify nociception but to render the patient functionally independent by modifying behaviour. Nevertheless, whether this was intended or not, patients treated using an operant model tend to report reduced levels of pain and require less medication; there also tend to be attendant cognitive changes, such as an increase in self-efficacy beliefs (Dolce 1987).

The role of cognitive factors in chronic pain patients should not be underestimated: Main and Waddell (1991) report a high incidence of catastrophizing thoughts, which was related to depressive symptoms, disability and work loss, even when severity of pain was controlled for. This also suggests possible tools for monitoring treatment and predicting response to this treatment. Further, Waddell *et al.* (1989) report a relationship between questions relating to illness behaviour and psychological distress, so that the belief that untreatable disease exists was related to high levels of distress. The direction of causation is unclear here, and there is likely to be an interactive effect. Importantly, Waddell *et al.* (1989) regard specific behaviours (disease conviction and lack of response to reassurance) as representing 'a psychological coping mechanism for individuals under stress'. What is not adequately explored is the extent to which this represents a coping mechanism which may be adaptive in the short term but gradually develops maladaptive features over time. Other cognitive changes associated with chronic pain include avoidance beliefs regarding physical activity (Waddell *et al.* 1993), work and so on, which in themselves may be reinforced. Memory biases, comparable to those well established in depressive patients, are also reported (Edwards *et al.* 1995), so that pain-related words are selectively processed by chronic pain patients. Furthermore, these biases remediate after recovery from chronic pain, which suggests that these biases are a consequence of the long-term nature of the pain rather than a specific, individual vulnerability factor. These cognitive biases also suggest methods of intervention other than the behavioural treatment programmes suggested above – that is, a cognitive-behavioural approach might be maximally effective. Pleasant imagery, for example, has been shown to benefit chronic pain patients, although the benefits are relatively short-lived (Raft et al. 1986). This may be in part the result of establishing a positive affective state, but may also act by interfering with negative cognitions and memory biases.

Assessment of the chronic pain patient, then, must include a broader range of features than would be included in acute pain assessment (Turk and Rudy 1990b), simply because the range of important factors is greater. The McGill Pain Questionnaire, for example (Melzack 1975), includes affective as well as sensory questions, and in chronic pain patients there is a greater frequency of use for the affective subgroup (Reading 1982). This may go some way to explaining the greater discrepancy between nurse and patient ratings of pain in chronic pain patients compared to acute pain patients (Teske et al. 1983). This suggests that clinical staff use incorrect or, more probably, insufficient cues to determine patient pain, and that this situation is exacerbated in chronic pain patients by the extended range of relevant factors, such as the increased importance of the patient's affective state. This is compounded by evidence that patients with no discernible physical pathology are assigned lower priority for pain medication by nurses (Taylor et al. 1984). This group of patients was also ascribed more negative personality and behavioural traits, so that the importance of a clearer understanding of the nature and genesis of the chronic pain patient must be emphasized on clinical as well as theoretical grounds. Undermedication for pain is a peculiar phenomenon (see Rachman and Arntz 1991): there is evidence that both patients and clinical staff (cf. Taylor et al. 1984) are responsible for this situation, and lack of appropriate education (either about the medication in the case of patients or the nature of chronic pain in the case of clinical staff) appears to be the primary cause of this. Of course, this is further confounded if a behavioural or cognitive-behavioural model of the genesis of chronic pain is accepted as in this case administration of medication provides further reinforcement. As a final point, however, it is well established that intermittent and delayed reinforcement is more difficult to extinguish, so that if chronic pain patients are simply assigned a lower priority to their medication requests (rather than ignored altogether and given medication at equal time intervals) these behaviours will become more difficult to break down.

Most of this section has emphasized the role of psychological factors in mediating pain response, in particular in chronic pain patients. This is not necessarily to deny the existence of a nociceptive element to the condition of chronic pain patients. Instead what is argued is that acute pain and chronic pain lie at extremes of a dimension of pain, with different factors being of varying importance at different points along this continuum. While the dimension is a temporal one, this is only because the importance of specific factors increases over time, rather than time from first injury being a defining feature of chronic pain per se. It is this misunderstanding of the nature of chronicity in pain patients which has led to inappropriate treatment and contributed to the sense of hopelessness and other cognitive changes which characterizes the chronic pain syndrome. The situation can be summarized by example: if a patient is admitted with low back injury, the initial pain will be primarily the result of nociception resulting from tissue damage, with psychological factors playing only a supplementary role. If this tissue damage does not resolve quickly, however, the behaviours which are adaptive in the short term (such as inactivity and medication request) become reinforced by environmental factors. Gradually these factors gain in importance, so that at some point (which cannot be defined as simply as, say, six months after injury) there may be no more discernible physical pathology but the pain behaviours persist, with attendant cognitive and affective biases developing as the condition progresses. The end point is the chronic pain syndrome. If this were the whole story it would be tempting to regard the pain as in some sense not real; this is crucially dangerous: it has already been argued that pain behaviour is the primary criterion for assessing whether or not someone is in pain. More exciting, however, is recent research (described briefly in previous sections) regarding the role of central neural plasticity. It is possible, then, that behavioural changes associated with pain that does not resolve are related to a shift in the primary site of nociception from the low back (in this example) to the spinal cord, where sensory fibres are sensitized, either by continued peripheral activity or, conceivably, by the behaviour of the subject. In a similar way to gate control theory, this conception provides us with a useful shorthand for understanding the interactive effects which contribute to the genesis of the chronic pain syndrome.

The final question is how this model can incorporate apparently disparate cases of persistent pain without attendant cognitive or behavioural changes (as opposed, here, to chronic pain), intermittent pain, cancer pain, rheumatoid arthritis, and so on. Advanced cancer, for example, is usually associated with severe pain, and there is a strong literature on the cognitive, affective and behavioural components of this (Barkwell 1991). Here the fact that the primary cause of the pain is a (potentially) terminal illness introduces an important feature not present in cases of, say, low back pain. While behavioural features are likely to develop in a similar way to the chronic pain patients described above, operant treatment programmes may be of limited value. This is because one implication of the suggestions made previously is that operant treatment reverses the progression along the time-line from acute to chronic pain. This may be associated with a reversal of semi-permanent changes in central pain information transmission fibres. In these cases, the original cause of the nociception is of secondary importance; in cancer pain, however, the cause of the pain remains of central importance, and indeed is important in determining the meaning ascribed to the pain by patients, and the attendant cognitive and affective changes. A similar story can be suggested for other degenerative conditions such as rheumatoid arthritis and multiple sclerosis, where pain remains an unresolved symptom (Indaco *et al.* 1994). In the case of chronic pain patients without degenerative disease the assumption made here is that in many cases healing does takes place at the site of original tissue damage, but that by this time behavioural and central nervous changes have taken place. These, however, are reversible, and this is patently not the case in patients with degenerative conditions. Special issues relating to cancer pain are discussed in more detail later (see pp. 124–5).

The interaction of factors modulating pain response, including the complexity of the physiological mechanisms allied to the variety of psychological, social and behavioural factors, necessitates the adoption of metaphors for these interactions if researchers across disciplines are to grasp the central issues (as is arguably the case in all science). Gate control theory provided one such shorthand for the interactive nature of the peripheral nervous system, as well as suggesting a physiological correlate of psychological mechanisms. Any adequate conception of chronic pain, and its relation to acute pain, requires a similar shorthand which emphasizes the progression from one to the other, so that the end points are apparently distinct but underpinned by the same mechanisms, albeit in different balances of importance. In turn, this allows for the advancement of theory and clinical practice in a way precluded by the adoption of simple mechanistic models.

Conclusion

Pain, as is the case with several other dynamic phenomena, has commonly been investigated as if a 'snapshot' taken at one point in time represents an adequate description of the phenomenon. Even attempts to take a series of such 'snapshots', such as including pre- and post-test measures, are inadequate, however, as they fail to take into account the role of intrapersonal developmental features which may act gradually over longer periods than are usually accounted for. Pain responses evolve over time, and are subject to a variety of influences from onset. The relative importance of these influences, however, varies considerably depending on what point in time one is considering. How this development takes place, and the relationship between psychological, behavioural and physiological factors (e.g. behavioural and central neural changes in chronic pain) represents a new area of study and one with enormous potential for development. Findings here are likely to be of crucial importance to the further development of our understanding, treatment and management of pain.

References

Barkwell, D.P. (1991) Ascribed meaning: a critical factor in coping and pain attenuation in patients with cancer-related pain. *Journal of Palliative Care*, 7: 5–14.

Biglan, A. (1991) Distressed behavior and its context. *Behavior Analyst*, 14: 157–69.

Bokan, J.A., Ries, R.K. and Katon, W.J. (1981) Tertiary gain and chronic pain. *Pain*, 10: 331–5.

Cohen, F. and Lazarus, R.S. (1973) Active coping processes, coping dispositions and recovery from surgery. *Psychosomatic Medicine*, 35: 375–89.

Craig, K.D. (1984) Psychology of pain. *Postgraduate Medical Journal*, 60: 835–40.

Dolce, J.J. (1987) Self-efficacy beliefs and disability beliefs in behavioural treatment of pain. *Behaviour Research and Therapy*, 25: 289–99.

Edwards, L.C., Pearce, S.A. and Beard, R.W. (1995) Remediation of pain-related memory bias as a result of recovery from chronic pain. *Journal of Psychosomatic Research*, 39: 175–81.

Egbert, L.D., Battit, G.E., Welch, C.E. and Bartlett, M.K. (1964) Reduction of postoperative pain by encouragement and instruction of patients: a study of doctor–patient rapport. *New England Journal of Medicine*, 270: 825–7.

Fordyce, W.E. (1984) Behavioral science and chronic pain. *Postgraduate Medical Journal*, 60: 865–8.

Fordyce, W.E., Fowler, R.S., Lehmann, J.F. and DeLateur, B.J. (1968) Some implications of learning in problems of chronic pain. *Journal of Chronic Disorders*, 21: 179–90.

Fordyce, W.E., Roberts, A.H. and Sternbach, R. (1985) The behavioral management of chronic pain: a response to critics. *Pain*, 22: 113–25.

Hilbert, R.A. (1984) The acultural dimensions of chronic pain: flawed reality construction and the problem of meaning. *Social Problems*, 31: 365–78.

Indaco, A., Iachetta, C., Nappi, C. and Socci, L. (1994) Chronic and acute pain syndromes in patients with multiple sclerosis. *Acta Neurologica*, 16: 97–102.

Jamison, R.N., Pairns, W.C. and Maxon, W.S. (1987) Psychological factors influencing recovery from outpatient surgery. *Behaviour Research and Therapy*, 25: 31–7.

Janis, I.L. (1958) *Psychological Stress: Psychoanalytic and Behavioral Studies of Surgical Patients*. New York: Wiley.

Jensen, M.P., Turner, J.A. and Romano, J.M. (1991) Self-efficacy and outcome expectancies: relationship to chronic pain coping strategies and adjustment. *Pain*, 44: 263–9.

Johnson, L.R., Magnani, B., Chan, V. and Ferrante, F.M. (1989) Modifiers of patient-controlled analgesia efficacy. I. Locus of control. *Pain*, 39: 17–22.

Johnston, M. and Carpenter, L. (1980) Relationship between pre-operative anxiety and post-operative state. *Psychological Medicine*, 10: 361–7.

Klos, D., Cummings, K.M., Joyce, J., Graichen, J. and Quigley, A. (1980) A comparison of two methods of delivering presurgical instructions. *Patient Counselling and Health Education*, 1: 6–13.

Krohne, H.W., Slangen, K. and Kleemann, P.P. (1996) Coping variables as predictors of perioperative emotional states and adjustment. *Psychology and Health*, 11: 315–30.

Lehmann, K.A., Ribbert, N. and Horrichs-Haermeyer, G. (1990) Postoperative patient-controlled analgesia with alfentanil: analgesic efficacy and minimum effective concentrations. *Journal of Pain and Symptom Management*, 4: 249–58.

Magnani, B., Johnson, L.R. and Ferrante, F.M. (1989) Modifiers of patient-controlled analgesia efficacy: II. Chronic pain. *Pain*, 39: 23–9.

Main, C.J. and Waddell, G. (1991) A comparison of cognitive measures in low back pain: statistical structure and clinical validity at initial assessment. *Pain*, 46: 287–98.

Martinez-Urrutia, A. (1975) Anxiety and pain in surgical patients. *Journal of Consulting and Clinical Psychology*, 43: 437–42.

Meilman, P.W. (1984) Chronic pain: the nature of the problem. *Journal of Orthopaedic and Sports Physical Therapy*, 5: 307–8.

Melzack, R. (1975) The McGill Pain Questionnaire: major properties and scoring methods. *Pain*, 1: 277–99.

Melzack, R. and Wall, P.D. (1982) *The Challenge of Pain*. Harmondsworth: Penguin.

Novy, D.M., Nelson, D.V., Francis, D.J. and Turk, D.C. (1995) Perspectives of chronic pain: an evaluative comparison of restrictive and comprehensive models. *Psychological Bulletin*, 118: 238–47.

Puntillo, K. and Weiss, S.J. (1994) Pain: its mediators and associated morbidity in critically ill cardiovascular patients. *Nursing Research*, 43: 31–6.

Rachman, S. and Arntz, A. (1991) The overprediction and underprediction of pain. *Clinical Psychology Review*, 11: 339–55.

Raft, D., Smith, R.H. and Warren, N. (1986) Selection of imagery in the relief of chronic and acute clinical pain. *Journal of Psychosomatic Research*, 30: 481–8.

Reading, A.E. (1982) A comparison of the McGill Pain Questionnaire in chronic and acute pain. *Pain*, 13: 185–92.

Roberts, A.H. and Reinhardt, L. (1980) The behavioral management of chronic pain: long-term follow-up with comparison group. *Pain*, 8: 151–62.

Smith, R.A., Wallston, B.S., Wallston, K.A., Forsberg, P.R. and King, J.E. (1984) Measuring desire for control of health care processes. *Journal of Personality and Social Psychology*, 47: 415–26.

Staub, E. and Kellett, D.S. (1972) Increasing pain tolerance by information about aversive stimuli. *Journal of Personality and Social Psychology*, 21: 198.

Suls, J. and Fletcher, B. (1985) The relative efficacy of avoidant and non-avoidant coping strategies. *Health Psychology*, 4: 249–88.

Taenzer, P., Melzack, R. and Jeans, M.E. (1986) Influence of psychological factors on post-operative pain, mood and analgesic requirement. *Pain*, 24: 331–42.

Taylor, A.G., Skelton, J.A. and Butcher, J. (1984) Duration of pain condition and physical pathology as determinants of nurses' assessments of patients in pain. *Nursing Research*, 33: 4–8.

Teske, K., Daut, R.L. and Cleeland, C.S. (1983) Relationships between nurses' observations and patients' self-reports of pain. *Pain*, 16: 289–96.

Thomas, V.J., Rose, F.D., Heath, M.L. and Flory, P. (1993) A multidimensional comparison of nurse and patient controlled analgesia in the management of acute postsurgical pain. *Medical Science Research*, 21: 379–81.

Thomas, V.J., Heath, M.L., Rose, F.D. and Flory, P. (1995) Psychological characteristics and the effectiveness of patient-controlled analgesia. *British Journal of Anaesthesia*, 74: 271–6.

Turk, D.C. (1994) Perspectives on chronic pain: the role of psychological factors. *Current Directions in Psychological Science*, 3: 45–8.

Turk, D.C. and Rudy, T.E. (1990a) Neglect factors in chronic pain treatment outcome studies: referral pattern, failure to enter treatment and attrition. *Pain*, 43: 7–25.

Turk, D.C. and Rudy, T.E. (1990b) Towards a comprehensive assessment of chronic pain: a multiaxial approach. *Behavior Research and Therapy*, 25: 237.

Turner, J.A. and Chapman, C.R. (1982) Psychological interventions for chronic pain: a critical review. *Pain*, 12: 1–46.

Virgil 'Georgics', no. 2.1.490, trans. R.A.B. Mynors (ed) (1994). Oxford: Clarendon Press.

Waddell, G., Pilowsky, I. and Bond, M.R. (1989) Clinical assessment and interpretation of abnormal illness behaviour in low back pain. *Pain*, 39: 41–53.

Waddell, G., Newton, M., Henderson, I., Somerville, D. and Main, C.J. (1993) A Fear-Avoidance Beliefs Questionnaire (FABQ) and the role of fear-avoidance beliefs in chronic low back pain and disability. *Pain*, 52: 157–68.

Wall, P.D. (1983) Pain as a need state. *Journal of Psychosomatic Research*, 27: 413.

Wallace, L.M. (1986) Pre-operative state anxiety as a mediator of psychological adjustment to and recovery from surgery. *British Journal of Medical Psychology*, 59: 253–61.

Wallace, L.M. (1987) Trait anxiety as a predictor of adjustment to and recovery from surgery. *British Journal of Clinical Psychology*, 26: 73–4.

Wilder-Smith, C.H. and Schuler, L. (1992) Postoperative analgesia: pain by choice? The influence of patient attitudes and patient education. *Pain*, 50: 257–62.

Wilson, J.F. (1981) Behavioral preparation for surgery: benefit or harm? *Journal of Behavioral Medicine*, 4: 79–102.

Wolfer, J.A. and Davis, C.E. (1970) Assessment of surgical patients' pre-operative emotional condition and post-operative welfare. *Nursing Research*, 19: 402–14.

CHAPTER 5

Personal, social and cultural factors

The inadequacy of pure sensory models of pain has resulted in an explosion of research examining the role of psychological and social factors in pain perception and response.

(Turk and Fernandez 1991: 17)

Summary

The experience of pain is the end result of a number of physiological, psychological, social and cultural factors; some are beginning to be known but there are probably others as yet unidentified. It is becoming clear that the interrelationships between these factors are a rich area of study.

In this chapter, the many diverse models constructed to account for individual differences in pain are sampled. These include models based on personality traits or types, and those based on cognition and learning. This is to some extent an artificial distinction except at the extremes of the nature/nurture argument, but it serves to lend some structure to the mass of information generated by the enormous number of studies in the area.

Introduction

Some explanatory models about pain have reached the public consciousness, as illustrated by the following example of a nurse talking to a postoperative patient, overheard on a hospital ward:

Nurse: Would you like some painkillers, Mrs X?
Patient: No, thank you.
Nurse: Don't be brave, now.
Patient: I'm not brave – I'm just not in pain.
Nurse: Ah, we find that some ladies have a high pain threshold. You're one of the lucky ones.
Patient: (*humbly*) Thank you.

If the nurse had been a behaviourist, she might have taken the first 'no' as denoting no pain and left it at that. As a cognitive-behaviourist, she might have been interested in the patient's interpretation of the sensation from her wound as not painful: expectation based on social learning? Had she been concerned with personality factors, she might have assumed that her patient was an introvert, or had high ego-strength. She might have looked for clues about the patient's behaviour in her sociocultural background (a stoical North European?). As it was, she settled for an uncritical 'people have different thresholds' explanation, suited to the circumstances. She had a pre-existing account of pain and fitted the patient's response to it. Such accounts are useful in confirming shared, culturally determined meanings, but they tend to offer explanations by hindsight rather than prediction. The following explanatory models have been constructed from social-scientific methods of inquiry and should at the very least permit prediction.

Behavioural science and pain

The kind of question that a pain researcher might ask includes: How are the ways that we deal with and express pain determined? There are many ways of answering such a question, including those derived from the study of individual differences. The interest of Fordyce and other behavioural scientists is not in predicting behaviour from personal traits, but in how pain behaviour is shaped by the interaction of the individual and the environment. Learning is the key concept in the behaviour and in its management (Fordyce *et al.* 1968; Fordyce 1984).

Both classical and operant conditioning have been implicated in the development of the pain response. Gentry and Bernal (1977) suggested that tissue damage/nociception could lead to a pain–tension–pain cycle by classical conditioning. Fordyce first applied the concepts of behavioural science to behaviour associated with chronic pain. He argued that behaviours which indicate the presence of pain are subject to the same factors that influence any behaviour. Fordyce commented on the influence of both classical and operant conditioning on behaviour, but focused on conditioning of operant behaviours by reinforcement. Some behaviours are respondent; they arise as the result of nociceptive stimuli. They include a variety of mental and physical responses such as local increases in muscle tension (guarding), attention focused on the pain and raised anxiety. These initially respondent behaviours may be followed by reinforcement such as care from others or pain-relieving medication, and thus become operants. Behaviour followed by a reinforcing consequence is likely to increase in frequency; behaviour followed by the absence of reinforcement is likely to decrease in frequency or to be extinguished altogether. Reinforcement may be positive – that is, behaviour is followed by a pleasant or satisfying event – or negative.

Negative reinforcement occurs when a behaviour is followed by the termination of an unpleasant or non-satisfying event. The efficacy of the conditioning is influenced by a number of factors, including the length of time the behaviour has been emitted (the longer the time, the more opportunities there are for reinforcement), the extent to which the environment is arranged to facilitate reinforcement, and the previous experience of the person, which will colour the expectation of reinforcement when behaviours are emitted.

Another view of the role of reinforcement in pain behaviour, hinted at by Wall (1979) when he conceptualized pain as an awareness of a need state, is that any behaviour resulting in or followed by a reduction in a need state (drive) is reinforced. Drive reduction is inherently reinforcing, so any behaviour leading to a reduction in pain level is likely to increase in frequency. This behaviour does not necessarily involve other people; resting and taking medication, for example, do not always attract attention from others, but are reinforced by the contingent reduction in pain.

These patterns of conditioned behaviour have been characterized in terms of 'gain' by some writers (e.g. Bokan *et al.* 1981). In this schema, primary (intrapersonal) gain is said to occur when pain behaviour results in rewarding consequences such as avoiding conflict. Secondary (interpersonal) gain is obtained from the environment, and includes obtaining care and nurturance from others. Tertiary (extrapersonal) gain is obtained by someone other than the patient, as when, for example, a partner gains in self-esteem through the caring role, or taking over the management of the household. Bokan *et al.* go on to point out the importance of considering the patient's social context in assessing and planning treatment regimens for pain.

Brena and Chapman (1985) suggested that a specific set of behaviours could arise from patterns of reinforcement in pain behaviour, the *learned pain syndrome*, which they characterized as the Five Ds:

♦ **D**ramatization of complaints
♦ **D**isuse (through diminution of activity)
♦ **D**rug misuse
♦ **D**ependency (learned helplessness, loss of competent coping skills)
♦ **D**isability (secondary impairments caused by inactivity)

The components of this model are present in Karoly and Jensen's (1987) Pain Context Model, in which pain is conceptualized as an information control/action system. The clinical features of chronic pain are explained thus:

1 Under the influence of reduced external stimulation and sensory or schema-driven processes, chronic pain patients tend to differentially monitor, encode and interpret bodily activities as distressing.

2 Chronic pain patients tend to develop self-defeating cognitive-behavioural control strategies, including the denial of responsibility/capability

for pain modulation, the pursuit of incompatible goals, and the schematic anticipation and avoidance of future suffering, leading to immobility-based atrophy (and more pain).

3 Self-defeating patterns and conceptual models become strengthened through contingent rewards.

These models were developed to explain features of chronic pain, but they could equally apply to intermittent pain such as that associated with migraine or arthritic conditions.

Fordyce's conceptualization of the role of learning is concerned with overt pain behaviour, not with subjective experience, and is essentially descriptive. However, many researchers since then have demonstrated the effect of learning on pain behaviour. Studies have, for example, demonstrated the influence of modelling (e.g. Fagerhaugh 1974; Thelen and Frye 1981; Violon and Giurgea 1984; Craig 1978), a relationship between spouse solicitousness and pain behaviour (e.g. Block *et al.* 1980; Flor *et al.* 1987), and the efficacy of behavioural principles in the management of pain (e.g. Keefe 1982; Moore *et al.* 1984; Turner and Romano 1984; Peters and Large 1990).

Fordyce's pioneering work on behavioural science and pain concerned itself with overt behaviour, and with 'unconscious' learning. Since then, and following on from his demonstration of learning principles in pain behaviour, interest in the relationship between pain and inner states such as cognition and mood has burgeoned, and with it an increasing emphasis on the awareness of adaptive and maladaptive behaviours as crucial in effecting change.

Cognitive-behavioural models and pain

Recent research has moved away from personality as a construct and from overt behaviour as the focus of interest, and has concentrated on cognitive variables as potential mediators of pain behaviour, and on identifying cognitive elements as agents of behaviour and behaviour change. This shift of focus has paralleled the spread of psychological models from chronic pain to pain associated with medical procedures, trauma and palliative care. The emphasis on cognitive and behavioural variables invites a shift away from a fundamentally individualistic psychology, as the social and cultural contexts in which such attributes develop play a central role in shaping them.

Cognitions are the means by which we make sense of and manage the world. As Barnlund (1976) put it:

It is tempting in the daily clash of words to forget that it is the perceived world – not the real world – that we talk about, argue about, laugh about, cry about. It is not scalpels and crosses and bedpans that regulate human affairs, but how people construe them that determines what they will think, how they will feel, and what they will do about them. . . . pain itself depends on the meaning attributed to physical incapacity. This meaning in turn reflects the past experiences and future expectations of the patient.

(Barnlund 1976: 717)

Cognition is 'the quality of knowing which includes perceiving, recognizing, conceiving, judging, sensing, reasoning and imagining' to quote the definition chosen by Weisenberg (1984: 162). In other words, the distinctive ways of construing the self, events in the world and the relationship between them. Traditionally, mental events were seen as belonging to one of three systems cognitive (thinking), affective (emotional) and connative (motivational). Here, no such distinctions are made; cognitions mediate affective and volitional schemata and behaviour, and vice versa. Even 'innate' responses such as startle to loud noise change over time and with the context of exposure; habituation or sensitization may occur, and the context of the exposure may imbue the stimulus with a range of meanings so that it invokes fear in some circumstances or for some people, and excitement in others. Strength of drive and tendency to persist are in part determined by the expectation of outcome.

Studies of cognition and pain have included a number of variables such as memory (e.g. Pincus *et al.* 1993), coping style (e.g. Cohen 1987), self-efficacy (Bandura 1977), locus of control (Rotter 1966), fear/anxiety (Bolles and Franslow 1980) and depression (Beck *et al.* 1979; Seligman *et al.* 1979). The common ground among these models is that although they may be characteristic of an individual and appear sometimes to be entrenched, there is an assumption that learning has played a part in their development and that they are amenable to modification by learning. Although they have often been studied in isolation, it is clear that there is considerable interrelatedness among them. A strong association has been shown for example, between chance external locus of control and the maladaptive coping strategy 'catastrophizing' (Härkäpää *et al.* 1996), between passive coping strategies and depression (Brown *et al.* 1989) and low self-efficacy and depression (Anderson *et al.* 1995).

The interrelatedness of many of the variables studied suggests that there may be other underlying factors. A thread running through many findings, for example, is the notion of control. Whether a sense of personal control over events is real or illusory, it appears to be a salient factor in the perception and management of pain and the concomitants of pain. Coping style is another related concept. It is frequently categorized by dimensions such as active/passive, internal/external, and high/low self-efficacy, for example, which have some elements in common and some which are construct-specific. There may be other underlying variables with wide-reaching associations with pain, but as yet there is no multidimensional model which attempts to incorporate them.

The direction of causality between pain and cognitive factors is not always clear. Pain may contribute to or confirm a sense of helplessness or a tendency to engage in catastrophic thoughts: that the suffering is unalterable, for example, and may itself be exacerbated by them. Helplessness and catastrophizing are considered by writers such as Beck (1976) and Seligman (1981) to be characteristic modes of thought in depression, which is another common concomitant of chronic pain, and one which may demonstrate reciprocal causality. Catastrophizing is also a common feature of anxiety.

Anxiety, depression and pain

Depression as a concomitant of chronic pain has been the subject of several studies (e.g. Boston *et al.* 1990; Anderson *et al.* 1995). Psychological models of depression include those based on behavioural/cognitive approaches, which assume an underlying faulty attributional style. Beck (1976) conceptualized the components of depression as negative thoughts, logical errors in thinking, and long-lasting attitudes or assumptions, developed over a period of years as a way of making sense of past experiences, and organized into depressogenic schemata.

Seligman (1981) presented a view of depression based on four fundamental premises:

1 The individual expects that a highly aversive state of affairs is likely (or a highly desired state of affairs is unlikely).
2 The individual expects to be able to do nothing about the likelihood of these events.
3 The individual possesses a maladaptive attributional style so that negative events tend to be attributed to internal, stable and global causes, and positive events to external, stable and specific causes.
4 The greater the certainty of the expected aversive state of affairs and the expected uncontrollability, the greater the strength of motivational and cognitive deficits. The greater the importance to the individual of the uncontrollable event, the greater will be the affective and self-esteem disruptions.

Becker *et al.* (1987) summarized the work of Rehm and others on faulty self-referent cognitions in depression:

◆ selective self-monitoring for negative events
◆ selective self-monitoring for immediate rather than long-term consequences of behaviour
◆ stringent self-evaluative standards
◆ inaccurate attributions

- deficient self-reinforcement
- excessive self-punishment.

Other cognitive/behavioural models of depression include those of Lewinsohn (1975), which considered the role of interpersonal interaction in depression and posited that depressed people tend to have poor social skills. They have a low rate of emission of interpersonal behaviours that elicit positive reinforcement.

Price (1991) suggested that depression evolved as a mechanism for inhibiting challenge in social groups. Depressed mood induces the adoption of the 'loser' role in social competition, the one-down position in a complementary relationship. In the sick role, the message conveyed to those seen as adversaries is 'I am sick and therefore no threat to you', and to supporters, 'I am sick and therefore out of action; stop pushing me into the arena to fight on your behalf.' The function of these messages is to inhibit challenge from 'adversaries' and elicit nurturant support from close others. Price and Gardner (1995) comment on the paradoxical power of depressed people over their supporters, and reiterate the views of Clarkin and Haas (1988) on the importance of the assessment of illness-related perceptions, cognitions and behaviours of the spouse and other family members in the understanding and management of depressive mood.

These views of depression as learned behaviour are interesting to the student of pain because they contain the elements of perceived powerlessness, low expectations of positive outcome, distorted cognitions and environmental reinforcement of maladaptive behaviour, all of which have been implicated in pain, and all of which are potentially remediable by behavioural or cognitive/behavioural means. Some authors have conceptualized chronic pain as masked or somatized depression, and others have discussed reciprocal causality (see Roy 1982) but the precise nature of the relationship between the two has yet to be illuminated.

The interrelationship between pain and fear/anxiety has also been investigated, in clinical and laboratory studies. Dougher *et al.* (1987) for example, investigated pain threshold and pain tolerance in the laboratory, under conditions of induced general anxiety, induced pain-specific anxiety, nonveridical exaggerated descriptions of the sensations produced by a pain stimulator, and a control condition. Results showed that only pain-specific anxiety enhanced pain responsivity for both males and females.

Osgood and Szyfelbein (1989) commented on a number of studies in which anticipation of burns dressing changes in children was associated with fear and anxiety, which 'undoubtedly magnifies pain perception of the child during the event'. The development of these emotional responses can be explained by classical conditioning: the painful procedure of dressing change is repeated often and at frequent intervals (two to three days) and paired with distinctive environmental cues (the nurse is gowned and masked, the procedure takes place in a clinic room, etc.).

Sanders (1985: 63) wrote that 'tissue damage and irritation can serve as an obvious aversive unconditioned stimulus, eliciting unconditioned neurophysiological, certain cognitive/subjective (e.g. fear), and gross motor (e.g. crying) pain responses'.

Philips (1987) has drawn attention to the limitations of conditioning models and the gate control theory in accounting for some aspects of chronic pain, and has considered the functional relationship between cognitions (e.g. expectations, beliefs and memory for past experiences) and avoidance behaviour in both pain and anxiety. Philips points out that avoidance is often extensive and complex in pain patients, and may encompass movement, stimulation, activity, social interactions and leisure pursuits.

It is suggested that avoidance behaviour plays a part in reducing a sense of control over pain and increasing the expectation that exposure will increase pain. As with phobic anxiety, avoidance may serve to maintain and augment pain. Philips (1987) demonstrated a relationship between avoidance of a stressful noise stimulus and increased sensitivity on subsequent exposure; that is, avoidance had a detrimental effect on stimulus tolerance. Philips argues that although avoidance behaviour is not associated with diminished pain, and therefore operant-conditioning models would predict that it would be extinguished, it is in fact maintained by accumulated beliefs and memories. Avoidance is driven by an expectation of pain increase following exposure.

Attention

Wall (1979) has argued that traumatic injury does not always result in pain initially, and that this phenomenon may have survival value in allowing the organism to escape from danger without being overwhelmed. With the majority of injuries, however, pain is a feature sooner or later. Pain in acute settings tends to have an urgent, unpleasant quality and to be difficult to ignore. The value for survival of these qualities is also evident where care of the wound or disease is paramount. The same attention-capturing quality is often reported in chronic pain, however, in which case not only is it non-useful but it may be positively detrimental. The 'hypochondriasis' identified as typical of some chronic pain patients in studies using scales such as the MMPI reflects, in part, hypervigilance about bodily sensations – that is, focused attention sharpened by anxiety. 'Continual vigilance and monitoring of noxious stimulation and the belief that it signals disease progression, may render even low intensity nociception less bearable' (Turk and Fernandez 1991: 24).

On the other side of the coin, the power of attention-diversion techniques in reducing pain experience has been reported in many studies (see for example Turk and Rennert 1981) and will be further discussed in Chapter 7.

Memory and pain

Memory for aspects of acute traumatic pain has clear survival value, and has been described and demonstrated in infants from around 14 months, who show anticipatory distress and avoidance behaviour in situations in which they have experienced pain (e.g. injections). Some authors have argued, however, that among the cognitive distortions implicated in chronic pain is selective self-referrent memory. Pincus *et al.* (1993) demonstrated that a group of chronic pain patients selectively recalled more pain-associated words than other word-types, but only for stimuli encoded with reference to themselves. Control subjects showed no difference in recall of word-types, regardless of the encoding condition. The authors suggested that the self-concept of pain patients, particularly the concept of themselves as pain patients, is responsible for the bias in recall for pain-associated information. Keefe and Williams (1989) report on a number of studies showing a tendency for recalled pain to be subject to systematic distortion; among the findings are that a group of chronic pain patients tended to over-estimate baseline pain after treatment, that rheumatoid arthritis patients recalled the intensity of a single episode of ischaemic pain better than a prolonged period of disease-related pain, and that women asked to recall aspects of labour pain two days post-partum systematically underestimated intensity. Eich *et al.* (1985) showed that current pain state influenced recall of pain intensity in a group of headache patients. Roche and Gijsbers (1986) found that mood at recall affected accuracy of memory, and Bryant (1993) in a study of 40 chronic pain patients before and after a six-week pain management programme, found that those who reported increased pain or depression over the course of the study overestimated their memory for initial pain or depression. Jamison *et al.* (1989) reported that a constellation of factors, emotional distress, conflict at home, reliance on medication and inactivity predicted overestimation of remembered pain intensity levels in chronic pain patients. While it is not possible to invoke a single explanatory system for these findings, the role of current mood, current pain, meaning and context in recall of pain merits further investigation, as do characteristics of the recalled episodes such as pain type and intensity, time-length, pattern and number. Morley (1993) has also suggested that memory for a pain experience is not unitary. Intensity and distress may be encoded or retrieved from memory somewhat differently from the sensory quality of the pain. Morley suggests that the separation of cognitive and somatosensory components of pain memory has advantages for survival; events laden with emotional intensity are richly represented in memory, and this would facilitate learning-from-experience.

As Pancyr and Genest (1993) have pointed out, there are several important reasons for studying memory for pain, including the fact that patients' recall of pain is used in both diagnosis and assessment of treatment interventions, and research instruments rely on pain memories when subjects are asked to compare their present pain with a pain memory. For these reasons, sources of systematic distortion of recall should be identified and accounted for.

Coping style and control

'Coping' is a complex of behaviours and is determined by a number of factors including perceived available resources (personal and situational), expectation of outcome and ascribed characteristics of the event to be coped with. Schüssler (1992) carried out empirical investigations on meaning as it impacts on chronic painful conditions, and demonstrated a relationship between ascribed meaning and outcome. Illness seen as *challenge* and illness as *value, acceptance* and *internal control* were related to mental well-being and adaptive coping. Illness seen as *enemy*, as *punishment*, as *relief* or as *strategy* was associated with psychological symptoms and maladaptive coping. Schüssler further related these constellations of meanings to 'emotion-focused' (passive) and 'problem-focused' (active) coping strategies. Coping strategies are patterns of behaviour aimed at managing stress; that is, intended to avoid or mitigate the consequences of a stressor (Cohen 1987). Crudely, emotion-focused strategies are those which concentrate on reducing anxiety and psychological discomfort (wishful thinking, denial, prayer) and problem-focused strategies are those which seek to change the stressful situation (information-seeking, undertaking therapeutic regimens). Coping style may be regarded as the preferred or typical strategy. Newman *et al.* (1990) have commented that it is unreasonable to expect coping strategies to be static over time; that the issues involved in coping with a discrete event are likely to be different from those in a constantly stressful situation; and that overall stress level may influence coping. Zautra and Manne (1992) have drawn attention to the fact that not all coping strategies may be useful or successful; some people persevere with strategies in the face of all evidence that their efforts are accomplishing nothing. Such behaviour has been variously described as immature or unrealistic coping. Vitiliano *et al.* (1990) found that appraisal of the stressful situation as changeable/ unchangeable impacted on psychological distress. In their study, patients who used problem-focused coping *and* saw their situation as alterable had less evidence of depression; this was not true of patients with similar coping styles but who saw their situation as unalterable.

Brown and Nicassio (1987) developed and tested the Vanderbilt Pain Management Inventory (VPMI) with a group of chronic pain patients. The inventory contained cognitive and behavioural items, and factor analysis showed that there were two factors: active coping and passive coping. Both factors had cognitive and behavioural items. Repeat testing at six months showed a relationship between passive coping at initial testing and pain, depression, helplessness, and lowered self-efficacy at second testing.

Active coping at initial testing predicted lower levels of depression and higher levels of self-efficacy six months on.

Newman *et al.* (1990) investigated coping patterns of people with rheumatoid arthritis, and showed that the stance people took toward their illness, their 'idiosyncratic pattern of coping' was related to level of disability, perception of pain and joint stiffness, and psychological well-being. Those with the best outcomes in these respects made the fewest adjustments to their illness, and did not attempt to use denial, seek social support or distract themselves from the consequences of their illness. These two studies are like many others; they sample coping behaviour at a point (or two points) in time and note the relationship between it and current illness factors. It may be that even if the coping strategies sampled are relatively fixed patterns of behaviour (which is by no means clear), their adaptive value will change over time and across situations. A longer-term sampling procedure is required to capture the dynamic features of coping and its relationships with pain and illness parameters.

Self-efficacy

Self-efficacy is something like confidence: it is the conviction or expectation that one is competent to perform certain behaviours successfully. Bandura (1989: 423) described efficacy beliefs as 'the product of a complex process of self-persuasion that relies on the cognitive processing of diverse sources of efficacy information conveyed enactively, vicariously, socially and physiologically'. He argued that the strength of the belief will determine whether one will emit and persist with a coping response, and how much effort will be put into it. In adverse situations, including those involving pain, self-efficacy beliefs affect how much stress and depression people feel, as well as their level of motivation.

> People who believe they can exercise control over potential threats do not conjure up apprehensive cognitions and, hence, are not perturbed by them. But those who believe they cannot manage potential threats experience high levels of anxiety arousal . . . they distress themselves and constrain and impair their level of functioning.
>
> (Bandura 1989: 419)

Self-efficacy is not a fixed attribute. It is learned through agencies such as mastery experiences (see for example Bandura *et al.* 1982). It is therefore liable to change over time and in different situations, and may be strengthened or weakened by factors such as vicarious experience (modelling), verbal persuasion, level of arousal and performance accomplishment. Studies by Jensen *et al.* (1991) and Council *et al.* (1988) have demonstrated a close association between self-efficacy beliefs and actual behaviour in pain management programmes. Dolce (1987) reviewed a number of clinical and experimental studies of the relationship between self-efficacy and the perception and management of pain, and concluded that behavioural interventions for pain may be refined when self-efficacy is taken into account; treatment programmes should include coping skills training. Anderson *et al.* (1995) have commented on the association between self-efficacy beliefs and treatment outcome variables in several studies of arthritis and chronic pain, and Anderson *et al.* (1991) showed significant post-treatment increases in Chronic Pain Self-efficacy Scale scores after a cognitive-behavioural treatment programme.

Finally Bandura (1989) has reviewed a number of studies which demonstrate a relationship between anxiety arousal and avoidance behaviour and perceived inefficacy, suggesting that there may also be indirect coeffects on pain from efficacy beliefs. This has been further elaborated by Thompson (1981) who argued that events perceived as potentially exceeding one's limit will arouse anticipatory anxiety and will provoke avoidance behaviour.

Locus of control

Locus of control, first propounded by Rotter (1966), is a concept related to self-efficacy. Put simply, it is that as a result of early experiences, some people come to believe that what happens to them is the result of their own actions. Success is seen as the reward of their effort and hard work, and failure is the consequence of poor effort or laziness. In Rotter's terms, these people have an *internal locus of control*. Other people come to believe that their own actions make very little difference to what happens to them; it is chance or fate that determines success or failure, good things or bad. These people have an *external locus of control*. Rotter proposed that internality was the result of the consistent use of reward and punishment for behaviour in childhood, and externality arose from inconsistency, so that predicting the result of one's actions was difficult or impossible. Locus of control was taken up with enthusiasm in the field of health psychology, and the concept has undergone several changes, including the division of external influences into 'chance' and 'powerful others' (Levenson 1981); and the development of a Multidimensional Health Locus of Control scale (MHLC) (Wallston *et al.* 1978) in which 'powerful others' came to mean health professionals, family and friends. The scale, the assumptions behind it, and its methodological weaknesses have been reviewed by Stainton Rogers (1991). It has proved to have poor predictive power in a number of studies, but variations of it continue to be developed, often disease- or condition-specific, as in the BPLC (back pain locus of control scale) (Vakkari 1990) depression locus of control scale (Whitman *et al.* 1987) and heart disease locus of control scale (O'Connell and Price 1985).

Whatever the difficulties are in producing a valid and reliable measure of it, the concept of locus of control has promise as a predictor of behaviour, including pain behaviour. It appears to be related to cognitive variables such as self-efficacy, attribution and coping style; perhaps it is an aspect of one or more of these models rather than a stand-alone concept, as has already been suggested. The imaginative research into the relationships between these variables has yet to be carried out.

Pain and personality

The relationship between pain and personality is both complex and vexed, largely because of difficulties of definition of 'personality'. Perhaps the most simple definition is 'distinctive personal character', which carries with it the implications of ways of behaving which are (a) relatively stable over time and in various situations, and (b) recognizable as being typical or predictable of that person. This way of looking at individual differences might lead to the question: Are there personality traits or types whose characteristics can be used to predict aspects of pain?

One way of exploring these individual differences is structural; the investigation of correlational relationships between behavioural acts, and the search for patterns among them. Eysenck (1947) construed four levels of behavioural organization: specific behaviours, habitual responses, traits and types. Habitual responses are specific behaviours which tend to recur under similar circumstances. A number of intercorrelated habitual acts forms a trait, and a constellation of intercorrelated traits forms a type. The type 'introvert' for example is made up of a number of traits including shyness, rigidity and persistence. Some theories of personality, including Eysenck's, assume an underlying biological blueprint. Galen based his humoral theory on the idea that one's characteristic ways of feeling, thinking and behaving were determined by the balance of four body fluids; choler, yellow and black bile, phlegm and blood. Choleric, melancholic, phlegmatic and sanguine are still familiar words used in describing personality 'types', and the notion that physiological and physical characteristics of the body are predictive of personality has re-emerged in various forms over the centuries, for example Kretschmer's (1936) body-build typology. These schemata are the ancestors of models such as those of Cattell and Eysenck, who used inventories composed of specific behaviours characteristic of certain traits to predict behaviour across a wide range of settings. Cattell (1943) constructed a personality questionnaire composed of a number of bipolar traits including dominance–submissiveness, excitability–insecurity, ego strength–neuroticism, each defined by clusters of typical responses, as follows:

Ego strength	*Neuroticism*
emotionally stable	emotional, dissatisfied
free of neurotic symptoms	showing a variety of neurotic symptoms

not hypochondriacal	hypochondriacal, plaintive
realistic about life	evasive, immature, autistic
unworried	worrying, anxious
steadfast, self-controlled	changeable
calm, patient	excitable, impatient
persevering and thorough	quitting, careless
loyal, dependable	undependable morally

Later factor analytic studies showed two independent factors, anxiety–integration/adjustment, and introversion–extraversion; the 'two fundamental dimensions of personality' as Eysenck (1970: 2 and 133–7) calls them (anxiety being equated with neuroticism). Eysenck's well-known series of scales (Maudsley Personality Questionnaire, Eysenck Personality Inventory (EPI), Eysenck Personality Questionnaire etc.) are based on the premise that the two fundamental dimensions are genetically determined and orthogonal, and have wide-ranging effects on very many aspects of behaviour including the way that sensory input is processed and learning style. As such, they have been used in a number of investigations of pain behaviour.

Lynn and Eysenck's (1961) study demonstrated a relationship between the trait of extraversion and tolerance for experimentally produced pain, and Eysenck's (1961) study of labour pain in primaparae showed a relationship between extraversion and pain behaviour. This apparently contradictory finding may reflect a difference between pain tolerance and pain expression; extraverts tolerate pain better in experimental conditions but describe it more exaggeratedly in a clinical situation. Bond and Pearson (1969), in a study of women with cancer, showed that those who had pain had high neuroticism scores. Those who also had high extraversion scores tended to ask for and receive more analgesics. As neuroticism as measured on the EPI has been related to levels of arousal, Bond and Pearson suggest that it is also related to sensitivity to pain. However, the danger in assessing factors like neuroticism in people while they are in pain is that there may be a response 'set'; what is being measured may be a reaction rather than an underlying factor. Evidence for this is given in a study by Hansen *et al.* (1995) in a health survey of 404 men and women aged 50, followed up at age 60 and 70. Using the Minnesota Multiphasic Personality Inventory (MMPI), a widely used instrument in which the traits are constructed from symptoms characteristic of psychiatric syndromes, they found elevated scores on the 'neurotic traits' of hypochondriasis, hysteria and depression in people with low back pain, but not in people without low back pain who later developed it. These results indicate that the MMPI profile followed the onset of pain rather than preceding it; it is not surprising that people in chronic pain should show evidence of lowered mood and preoccupation with bodily symptoms. The illogic of attempting to identify 'profiles' of pain patients in this way, together with the variability and inconsistency of the profiles identified, and the contradictory and inconsistent findings of studies predicting treatment outcomes from the profiles, has been commented on by Turk and Rudy (1987). See also Main *et al.*'s (1991) critique of the MMPI and pain.

Other models of personality, derived from psychoanalytic studies, include traits or constellations of behaviours developed during certain critical periods, often as defences against anxiety. The 'pain-prone personality' described by Engel (1959) is such a one. Engel argues that the psychic experience of pain develops from what was originally a reflex; a basic mechanism for protection from injury, triggered by noxious input from peripheral receptors. As psychic organization develops, there is no longer a need for peripheral stimulation to initiate pain. Pain becomes a part of our concepts of good and bad, reward and punishment, and other facets of interpersonal relationships such as mechanisms for dealing with aggression and guilt, although the extent to which it is employed as a mediator is a matter of individual difference. It is the link between pain, guilt and aggression which plays an important part in early family relationships, and which may lead to pain-proneness. In Engel's terms, the 'pain-prone' person is characterized by some of the following traits: excessive guilt, and a predisposition to use pain to atone for guilt, a strong unfulfilled aggressive drive, a history of suffering and defeat, with intolerance of success, the use of pain as a replacement for loss when a relationship is threatened, and a tendency to masochistic sexual development. Engel distinguishes between the 'pain-prone' person, who tends to have repeated episodes of pain, and the person with chronic pain. Carlsson's (1986) study supports this view and argues that chronic pain equates to masked depression, although whether the depression is pre-existing or reactive is not clear. Engel's model contains much food for thought about the influence of early experience on later behaviour, but there is no empirical evidence to support it.

A different view of 'type' has been taken by Brena and Koch (1975) in investigating the relationship between behaviour and tissue pathology in pain patients. Their Emory Pain Estimate Model (EPEM) provides operational definitions of four types of chronic pain patients. Medical data, a mixture of functional assessment and pathology, are rated on a 1–10 horizontal scale of severity by a physician. Scoring guidelines are given. Behavioural scores are obtained from patient self-report on a paper-and-pencil test, and are a compound of estimated activity levels, drug usage and personality variables. They are also scored 1–10 and entered on a scale which crosses the midline of the pathology scale at right angles, thus generating four cells:

1 High pain behaviour with low tissue pathology – Pain amplifiers.
2 Low pain behaviour with low tissue pathology – Pain verbalizers.
3 High pain behaviour with high tissue pathology – Chronic sufferers.
4 Low pain behaviour with high tissue pathology – Pain reducers.

The suggestion is that different treatment strategies should be used for the four types of patients identified by the EPEM scores. There is no evidence that the scales are orthogonal, however, and the scoring and aggregation of so many different types of data on to single scales is questionable, as is the idea of identifying types of people by this method, rather than types of reaction or behaviour. Brena and Koch (1975) do not comment on whether the types they identified are the result of innate predisposition or learning, as their purpose is to tailor treatments to the patients as they present, rather than concern themselves with how the behaviour developed. For other theorists, however, the focus of interest is on the context in which pain behaviour develops.

Social and cultural influences and pain

If, as Wall (1977) and others have suggested, one function of pain behaviour is to signal that there is a problem and to solicit help, then learning socially and culturally appropriate behaviour is clearly crucial. Craig (1978), Fagerhaugh (1974), Helman (1990) and others have written on the role of social learning in pain, shown in experimental studies and in the family, in social and cultural groups and the hospital or clinic. Helman used case histories and anthropological data to defend the propositions that not all social or cultural groups may respond to pain in the same way; that how people perceive and respond to pain, both in themselves and others, can be largely influenced by their cultural background; and that how and whether people communicate their pain to health professionals and to others can also be influenced by social and cultural factors. Melzack and Wall (1982: 16–19) have highlighted the wider social and cultural influences on pain in their commentary on the Indian hook-swinging ceremony and Nepalese sherpas; Zborowski (1952) and Winsberg and Greenlick (1967) have demonstrated ethnic differences in pain behaviour and have shown that there is a large learned component.

Lambert *et al.* (1960) demonstrated the power of group affiliation in a study in which Jewish women increased their pain tolerance levels after being told that their religious group tolerated pain less well than others. The meaning of these results is not clear. It is possible that the women were feeling the same level of pain but choosing not to disclose it. Alternatively, their reactions to the misinformation might have coloured their experience of the pain. Bates (1987) suggested that the learned component of pain behaviour is not just about overt acts and social appropriateness. She proposed a biocultural model, in which she argued that social and cultural learning shapes not only the outward behaviour but also the physiological component of pain, through the influence of the descending control mechanisms in gate control theory. Bates pointed out that social learning is instrumental in the development of meanings for and attitudes to pain. These learned values and attitudes affect attention to painful stimuli and memory for pain experiences. According to the gate control theory, attention, memory, attitudes and values are among the cognitive factors which influence psychophysiological functioning via descending pathways from higher cortical centres to the spinal cord.

Conclusion

This broad sweep of personal, social and cultural influences on pain contains some recurring themes. Concepts such as meaning and control have been shown to be related to pain, anxiety, depression and motivation, and coping styles. The direction of causality between these attributes and pain is by no means clear; they impact on, and are impacted on by, pain. They may be regarded as personal traits, but there is much evidence that they are acquired by learning and are subject to modification by learning. The very process of learning culture-appropriate pain behaviour may shape physiological responses. The survival advantages of captured attention and vivid emotional aspects of pain memory may also help to enhance and maintain pain in circumstances where inactivity, avoidance and low self-efficacy prevail. The complexities of the interrelationships between these intra- and interpersonal factors are only now beginning to be investigated.

References

Anderson, K.O., Edwards, W.T., Peeters-Asdourian, C., Dowds, B.N. and Pelletz, R. (1991) Development and initial validation of a self-efficacy scale to measure efficacy beliefs in people with chronic pain. Poster presented at the annual meeting of the American Pain Society, New Orleans.

Anderson, K.O., Dowds, B.N., Pelletz, R.E., Edwards, W.T. and Peeters-Asdourian, C. (1995) Development and initial validation of a scale to measure self-efficacy beliefs in patients with chronic pain. *Pain*, 63: 77–84.

Bandura, A. (1977) Self-efficacy: toward a unifying theory of behaviour change. *Psychological Review*, 84: 191–215.

Bandura, A. (1986) *Social Foundations of Thought and Action: A Social Cognitive Theory.* Englewood Cliffs, NJ: Prentice-Hall.

Bandura, A. (1989) Perceived self-efficacy in the exercise of personal agency. *The Psychologist*, 10: 411–24.

Bandura, A., Reese, L.B. and Adams, N.E. (1982) Microanalysis of action and fear arousal as a function of different levels of perceived self-efficacy. *Journal of Personality and Social Psychology*, 43: 5–21.

Barnlund, D.C. (1976) The mystification of meaning: doctor–patient encounters. *Journal of Medical Education*, 51: 716–25.

Bates, M. (1987) Ethnicity and pain: a biocultural model. *Social Science and Medicine*, 24: 47–50.

Beck, A.T. (1976) *Cognitive Therapy and the Emotional Disorders.* New York: International Universities Press.

Beck, A.T., Rush, A.J., Shaw, B.F. and Emery, G. (1979) *Cognitive Therapy of Depression.* New York: Guilford.

Becker, R.E., Heimberg, R.G. and Bellack, A.S. (1987) *Social Skills Training for Depression*. Oxford: Pergamon Press.

Block, A.R., Kremer, E.F. and Gaylor, M. (1980) Behavioral treatment of chronic pain: variables affecting treatment efficacy. *Pain*, 8: 367–75.

Bokan, J.A., Ries, R.K. and Katon, W.J. (1981) Tertiary gain and chronic pain. *Pain*, 10: 331–5.

Bolles, R.C. and Franslow, M.S. (1980) A perceptual/defensive/recuperative model of fear in pain. *Behaviour and Brain Sciences*, 3: 291–323.

Bond, M.R. and Pearson, I.B. (1969) Psychological aspects of pain in women with advanced cancer of the cervix. *Journal of Psychosomatic Research*, 13: 13–19.

Boston, K., Pearce, S.A. and Richardson, P.H. (1990) The Pain Cognitions Questionnaire. *Journal of Psychosomatic Research*, 34: 103–9.

Brena, S.E. and Chapman, S.L. (1985) Acute vesus chronic pain states: the 'Learned Pain Syndrome'. *Clinics in Anesthesiology*, 3: 41–55.

Brena, S.E. and Koch, D.L. (1975) The 'Pain Estimate' model for quantification and classification of pain states. *Anesthesiology Review*, 2: 8–13.

Brown, G.K. and Nicassio, P.M. (1987) Development of a questionnaire for the assessment of active and passive coping strategies in chronic pain patients. *Pain*, 31: 53–64.

Brown, G.K., Nicassio, P.M. and Wallston, K.A. (1989) Pain coping strategies and depression in Rheumatoid Arthritis. *Journal of Consulting and Clinical Psychology*, 57: 652–7.

Bryant, R.A. (1993) Memory for pain and affect in chronic pain patients. *Pain*, 54: 347–51.

Carlsson, A.M. (1986) Personality characteristics of patients with chronic pain in comparison with normal controls and depressed patients. *Pain*, 25: 373–82.

Cattell, R.B. (1943) The description of personality. *Psychological Review*, 50: 539–94.

Clarkin, J.F. and Haas, G.L. (1988) Assessment of affective disorders and their interpersonal context, in J.F. Clarkin and G.L. Haas (eds) *Affective Disorders and the Family*. New York: Guilford Press.

Cohen, F. (1987) Measurement of coping, in S.V. Kaol and C.L. Cooper (eds) *Stress and Health: Issues in Health Methodology*. New York: John Wiley & Sons, Inc.

Council, J.R., Ahern, D.K., Follick, M.J. and Kline, C.L. (1988) Expectancies and functional impairment in chronic low back pain. *Pain*, 33: 323–31.

Craig, K.D. (1978) Social modelling influences on pain, in R.A. Sternbach (ed.) *The Psychology of Pain*. New York: Raven Press.

Dolce, J.J. (1987) Self-efficacy and disability beliefs in the behavioural treatment of pain. *Behaviour Research and Therapy*, 25: 289–99.

Dougher, M.J., Goldstein, D. and Leight, K.A. (1987) Induced anxiety and pain. *Journal of Anxiety Disorders*, 1: 259–64.

Eich, E., Reeves, J.L., Jaeger, B. and Graf-Radford, S.B. (1985) Memory for pain: relation between past and present pain intensity. *Pain*, 23: 375–9.

Engel, G.L. (1959) Psychogenic pain and the pain prone patient. *American Journal of Medicine*, 26: 900–18.

Eysenck, H.J. (1947) *The Dimensions of Personality*. London: Kegan Paul.

Eysenck, H.J. (1970) *The Structure of Human Personality*. London: Methuen.

Eysenck, S.B. (1961) Personality and pain assessment in childbirth, of married and unmarried mothers. *Journal of Mental Sciences*, 107: 417–30.

Fagerhaugh, S. (1974) Pain expression on a burn care unit. *Nursing Outlook*, 22: 645–50.

Flor, H., Kerns, R.D. and Turk, D.C. (1987) The role of the spouse in the maintenance of chronic pain. *Journal of Psychosomatic Research*, 31: 251–60.

Fordyce, W.E. (1984) Behavioural science and chronic pain. *Postgraduate Medical Journal*, 60: 865–8.

Fordyce, W.E., Fowler, R.S., Lehmann, J.F. and DeLateur, B.J. (1968) Some implications of learning in problems of chronic pain. *Journal of Chronic Disorders*, 21: 179–90.

Gentry, W.D. and Bernal, G. (1977) Chronic pain, in R. Williams and W.D. Gentry (eds) *Behavioural Approaches to Medical Treatment*. Cambridge, MA: Ballinger.

Hansen, F.R., Biering-Sorensen, F. and Schroll, M. (1995) Minnesota Multiphasic Personality Inventory profiles in persons with or without low back pain. *Spine*, 20: 2716–20.

Härkäpää, K., Järvikoski, A. and Vakkari, T. (1996) Locus of control beliefs in back pain patients. *British Journal of Health Psychology*, 1: 51–63.

Helman, C.G. (1990) Pain and culture, in C.G. Helman, *Culture, Health and Illness*. Oxford: Butterworth-Heinemann.

Jamison, R.N., Sbrocco, T. and Parris, W.C.V. (1989) The influence of physical and psychosocial factors on accuracy of memory for pain in chronic pain patients. *Pain*, 37: 289–94.

Jensen, M.P., Turner, J.A. and Romano, J.M. (1991) Self-efficacy and outcome expectancies: relationship to chronic pain coping strategies and adjustment. *Pain*, 44: 263–9.

Karoly, P. and Jensen, M.P. (1987) *Multimethod Assessment of Chronic Pain*. New York: Pergamon Press.

Keefe, F.J. (1982) Behavioural assessment and treatment of chronic pain: current status and future trends. *Journal of Consulting and Clinical Psychology*, 50: 896–911.

Keefe, F.J. and Williams, D.A. (1989) New directions in pain assessment and treatment. *Clinical Psychology Review*, 9: 549–68.

Lambert, W.E., Libman, E. and Poser, E.G. (1960) Effect of increased salience of membership group on pain tolerance. *Journal of Personality*, 28: 350–7.

Levenson, H. (1981) Differentiating among internality, powerful others and chance, in H.M. Lefcourt (ed.) *Research with the Locus of Control Construct, vol. 1: Assessment Methods*. New York: Academic Press.

Lewinsohn, P.M. (1975) The behavioural study and treatment of depression, in M. Hersen, R.M. Eisler and P.M. Miller (eds) *Progress in Behaviour Modification 1*. New York: Academic Press.

Lynn, R. and Eysenck, H.J. (1961) Tolerance for pain, extraversion and neuroticism. *Perceptual and Motor Skills*, 12: 161–2.

Main, C.J., Evans, P.J.D. and Whitehead, R.C. (1991) An investigation of personality structure and other psychological features in patients presenting with low back pain: a critique of the MMPI, in M.R. Bond, J.E. Charlton and C.J. Woolf (eds) *Proceedings of the VIth Congress on Pain*. Amsterdam: Elsevier.

Melzack, R. and Wall, P. (1982) *The Challenge of Pain*. Harmondsworth: Penguin.

Moore, M.E., Berk, S.N. and Nypaver, A. (1984) *Archives of Physical Medicine and Rehabilitation*, 65: 356–61.

Morley, S. (1993) Vivid memory for 'everyday' pains. *Pain*, 55: 55–62.

Newman, S., Fitzpatrick, R., Lamb, R. and Shipley, M. (1990) An analysis of coping patterns in Rheumatoid Arthritis, in L.R. Schmidt, P. Schwenkmezger,

J. Weinman and S. Maes (eds) *Theoretical and Applied Aspects of Health Psychology.* Amsterdam: Harwood Academic.

O'Connell, J.K. and Price, J.H. (1985) Development of a heart disease locus of control scale. *Psychological Reports,* 56: 159–64.

Osgood, P.F. and Szyfelbein, S.K. (1989) Management of burn pain in children. *Pediatric Clinics of North America,* 36: 1001–12.

Pancyr, G. and Genest, M. (1993) Cognition and pain experience, in K.S. Dobson and P.C. Kendall (eds) *Psychopathology and Cognition.* San Diego, CA: Academic Press.

Peters, J.L and Large, R.G. (1990) A randomised control trial evaluating in- and outpatient pain management programmes. *Pain,* 41: 283–93.

Philips, H.C. (1987) Avoidance behaviour and its role in sustaining chronic pain. *Behaviour Research and Therapy,* 25: 273–9.

Pincus, T., Peace, S. and McLelland, A. (1993) Self-referential selective memory in pain patients. *British Journal of Clinical Psychology,* 32: 365–74.

Price, J.S. (1991) Homeostasis or change? A systems theory approach to depression. *British Journal of Medical Psychology,* 64: 331–44.

Price, J.S. and Gardner, R. (1995) The paradoxical power of the depressed patient: a problem for the ranking theory of depression. *British Journal of Medical Psychology,* 68: 193–206.

Price, J.S., Sloman, L., Gardner, R., Gilbert, P. and Rohde, P. (1994) The social competition hypothesis of depression. *British Journal of Psychiatry,* 164: 309–15.

Roche, P.A. and Gijsbers, K. (1986) A comparison of memory for induced ischaemic pain and chronic rheumatoid pain. *Pain,* 25: 337–43.

Rotter, J.B. (1966) Generalised expectancies for internal versus external control of reinforcement. *Psychological Monographs,* 80 (609): 1.

Roy, R. (1982) Many faces of depression in patients with chronic pain. *International Journal of Psychiatry in Medicine,* 12: 109–19.

Sanders, S.H. (1985) The role of learning in chronic pain states. *Clinics in Anaesthesiology,* 3: 57–73.

Schüssler, G. (1992) Coping strategies and individual meanings of illness. *Social Science and Medicine,* 34: 427–32.

Seligman, M.E.P. (1981) A learned helplessness point of view, in L.P. Rehm (ed.) Behavior Therapy for Depression. New York: Academic Press.

Seligman, M.E.P., Abramson, L.Y., Semmel, A. and von Baeyer, C. (1979) Depressive attributional style. *Journal of Abnormal Psychology,* 88: 242–7.

Stainton Rogers, W. (1991) *Explaining Health and Illness: An Exploration of Diversity.* Hemel Hempstead: Harvester Wheatsheaf.

Thelen, M.H. and Frye, R.A. (1981) The effect of modeling and selective attention on pain tolerance. *Journal of Behavior Therapy and Experimental Psychiatry,* 12: 225–9.

Thompson, S.C. (1981) Will it hurt less if I can control it? A complex answer to a simple question. *Psychological Bulletin,* 90: 89–101.

Turk, D.C. and Fernandez, E. (1991) Pain: a cognitive-behavioural perspective, in M. Watson (ed.) *Cancer Patient Care: Psychosocial Treatment Methods.* Cambridge: BPS Books.

Turk, D.C. and Rennert, K.S. (1981) Pain and the terminally-ill cancer patient: a cognitive and social learning perspective, in H. Sobel (ed.) *Behaviour Therapy in Terminal Care: A Humanistic Approach.* Cambridge, MA: Ballinger.

Turk, D.C. and Rudy, T.E. (1987) Towards a comprehensive assessment of chronic pain patients. *Behaviour Research and Therapy*, 25: 237–49.

Turner, J. and Romano, J.M. (1984) Evaluating psychologic interventions for chronic pain: issues and recent developments, in C. Benedetti, C.R. Chapman and G. Moricca (eds) *Advances in Pain Research and Therapy*, vol. 7. New York: Raven Press.

Violon, A. and Giurgen, D. (1984) Familial models for chronic pain. *Pain*, 18: 199–203.

Vakkari, T. (1990) 'Chronic low back pain and health locus of control', Masters thesis, University of Helsinki and used as a source in K. Härkäpää, A. Järvikoski and T. Vakkari (1996) Locus of control beliefs in back pain patients. *British Journal of Health Psychology*, 1: 51–63.

Vitiliano, P.P., DeWolfe, D.J., Maiuro, R.D., Russo, J. and Katon, W. (1990) Appraised changeability of a stressor as a modifier of the relationship between coping and depression: a test of the hypothesis of fit. *Journal of Personality and Social Psychology*, 59: 582–92.

Wall, P.D. (1977) Why do we not understand pain? in R. Duncan and M. Weston-Smith (eds) *Encyclopaedia of Ignorance*, vol. 2, pp. 361–8. Oxford: Pergamon Press.

Wall, P.D. (1979) On the relation of injury to pain. The John J. Bonica Lecture. *Pain*, 6: 253–64.

Wallston, K.A., Wallston, B.S. and DeVellis, R. (1978) The development of the multidimensional health locus of control (MHLC) scales. *Health Education Monographs*, 6: 161–70.

Weisenberg, M. (1984) Cognitive aspects of pain, in P.D. Wall and R. Melzack (eds) *Textbook of Pain*. New York: Churchill Livingstone.

Wener, A. and Rehm, H.P. (1975) Depressive affect: a test of behavioural hypotheses. *Journal of Abnormal Psychology*, 84: 221–7.

Whitman, L., Desmond, S.M. and Price, J.H. (1987) Development of a depression locus of control scale. *Psychological Reports*, 60: 583–9.

Winsberg, B. and Greenlick, M. (1967) Pain responses in negro and white obstetrical patients, in M. Weisenberg (ed.) *Pain: Clinical and Experimental Perspectives*. St Louis, MO: C.V. Mosby.

Zautra, A.J. and Manne, S.L. (1992) Coping with Rheumatoid Arthritis: a review of a decade of research. *Annals of Behavioural Medicine*, 14: 31–9.

Zborowski, M. (1952) Cultural components in response to pain. *Journal of Social Issues*, 8: 16–30.

CHAPTER 6

Measurement

Measurement refers to application of some metric to a specific element, usually intensity, of pain. Assessment is a much broader endeavour which encompasses the measurement of the interplay of different factors on the experience of pain

(McGrath and Unruh 1987: 74)

Summary

In the first section of this chapter, some of the issues in pain assessment and measurement are considered, with a selective, critical account of some common types of assessment tools and examples of their use drawn from the research literature. In the second section, the special problems of assessing pain in children are considered and an overview of measurement and assessment tools is given.

Why measure pain?

There are several reasons why the objective and systematic assessment of pain is necessary. In acute pain the object of assessment might be to judge the need for, or effectiveness of, analgesic medication; in chronic pain, the focus is more often on the effect of the pain on function, and on the progress and outcome of therapeutic interventions. Some measures require comparisons between current and usual pain, so that memory for pain is also being assessed. Karoly (1985) has suggested that among the aims of assessment for chronic pain are:

♦ to determine patient readiness for treatment
♦ to prioritize the foci of intervention
♦ to quantify the disruptiveness of the problem
♦ to assess the nature and adjustive impact of the patient's implicit pain theory.

These aims serve the purposes of informing and guiding interventions. Roth *et al.* (1990) identified a number of purposes of functional assessment which could be used to guide a selection of instruments for acute and chronic pain; among them are:

- to provide objective and quantitative measures of patient function
- to monitor changes in clinical status
- to guide management decisions
- to evaluate treatment efficacy
- to prevent additional disability
- to predict prognosis
- to estimate care requirements
- to determine compensation.

These purposes of assessment are also concerned with facilitating clinical decision-making, and suggest a multidimensional approach with emphasis on psychosocial factors rather than the single-scale techniques derived from laboratory studies. Increasingly, researchers in pain are using assessment tools which contain questions designed to assess elements of pain such as attitudes, meaning, emotional loading (for example, the Pain Discomfort Scale (Jensen et al. 1991), Pain Disability Index (Tait et al. 1990), Pain Anxiety Symptoms Scale (McCracken et al. 1992)); some researchers are using combinations of scales in an attempt to capture the complexities of pain (for example Williams and Keefe 1991). This has led some to suggest that assessment tools should be not merely reliable, valid and useful, but capable of generating quantifiable data which are amenable to multivariate analysis. This is an arguable point of view; the purpose for which the information is being gathered should determine the types of data required, and while it may be argued that clinical assessment should be no less rigorous than assessment carried out for research purposes, it is a mistake to equate rigour with numeracy, especially where linearity is a questionable assumption and oversimplification of complex multidimensional systems inevitably leads to error.

Can pain be measured?

One set of problems with the measurement of pain is technical, and is concerned with attempts to fit dynamic and complex events into simplistic numerical models. This has resulted in the generation of spurious numerical data, the assumption of linearity in scaling techniques, and the acceptance of questionable ideas about relationships between some aspects of pain – e.g. intensity and distressfulness – which have been treated as independent in some studies and conflated in others.

A second set of problems concerns the debate about what is being measured – a private experience or the public manifestation of it? One view is that the direct measurement of the experience of pain is not possible; we can assess pain behaviour only by observation or self-report, or look for physiological correlates of the pain experience, in the hope that there is close correspondence between the experience and the behaviour and/ or the experience and the physiology. Some writers have suggested that the outward expression and inner experience of pain are so intimately inter-related as to be indistinguishable for all practical purposes. Bates (1987) has argued that sociocultural influences may affect the perceptual component of pain. Thus both the perception of pain and its outward manifestations are learned during cultural group experiences. Experimental studies have shown that social modelling and group pressure influence pain tolerance levels, for example Koopman *et al.* (1984) and Lipton and Marbach (1984). Unless tolerance is a public display unrelated to the underlying experience, or is consciously deceptive, it must be concluded that the experience itself is moderated by social influences, and from this it may be argued that the physiological substrate of the experience is too, as Bates (1987) has proposed. That these influences are cultural (learned) rather than racial (genetic) is supported by studies such as that carried out by Winsberg and Greenlick (1975) on pain behaviour associated with labour in black and white women. Differences in pain behaviour and self-report of pain were related to age and parity, but when social class and cooperativeness were controlled for, there were no differences related to race. The nature of the learned com-ponent of pain is illuminated by Greenwald's (1991) study with patients from different ethnic groups, recently treated for forms of cancer known to cause pain. Greenwald used a graphical rating scale and the McGill Pain Questionnaire (MPQ), and found no significant differences between the groups for levels of pain sensation, but the affective component of the MPQ (such as the interpretation of pain as frightening) did vary between the groups.

Further evidence for the intimate interrelationship between pain behavi-our and experience was given by Syrjala and Chapman (1984). They reported on studies in which, when patients were requested to inhibit their facial expressions of pain, their autonomic and self-reported pain responses also decreased. When subjects were asked to exaggerate their facial expressions of pain, their subjective pain reports and autonomic responses increased. Syrjala and Chapman suggested that these expressive pain behaviours have a self-regulatory function; they modulate both the subjective experience of pain and its physiological concomitants.

Fordyce (1984; Fordyce *et al.* 1985) has dealt with the complexities of the relationship between pain experience and pain behaviour by concentrat-ing on the behaviour – the directly observable part of the picture. Even so, he commented that although behavioural treatments for chronic pain are intended to reduce the *disability* associated with the pain, large numbers of patients report decreases in pain following the application of such pro-grammes (Fordyce *et al.* 1985).

Examples such as these led R. Chapman (1984) to follow the philosoph-ical tradition and argue that the notion of pain as a private experience is flawed and is fading away. Pain is rightly regarded as 'a multidimensional phenomenon . . . increasingly measured, studied and controlled clinically, as a pattern of behaviour. As such, it can be considered objective rather than subjective' (1984: 1274).

Objectivity in pain measurement and assessment provides some interesting challenges, as has already been mentioned. Measures need to be *reliable* in that their internal consistency and test-retest consistency have been established, *valid* inasmuch as they are congruent with other measures or observations of behavioural events commonly accepted as denoting pain, and *sensitive*, in that they are a precise reflection of magnitude and change in what they are measuring. Crude test-retest reliability is often emphasized as an important test characteristic, but it may be achieved at the expense of sensitivity, as when a small number of options are presented (e.g. mild, moderate, severe) which will mask all but the grossest changes.

Measurement/assessment: what is measured?

The problem of what is being measured has been compounded by an over-concentration on the negative aspects of pain behaviour in research literature and clinical practice. This arose from the pioneering work of Fordyce, who devised treatment schedules based on operant conditioning for chronic pain patients, many of whom had longstanding and apparently intractable problems. The focus of attention in these schedules was on the extinction of the maladaptive behaviour by non-reinforcement, and as is well known, it has proved to be very effective. The techniques are used widely, and are often life-transforming. It is perhaps unfortunate, however, that what most people have come to understand by pain behaviour has been defined in so negative a way (see Fordyce 1984; Block 1991; Schmidt 1991, for a debate on what constitutes 'classic' pain behaviour).

One view of pain behaviour is that it is essentially a neutral concept; it is any and every outward manifestation of the inner, subjective state, and includes completing questionnaires and other assessment tools, and responses in clinical interviews. The other view, propounded by Fordyce and others, is that pain behaviour is a set of indicators of pain and suffering, whose function is to elicit help, and which is appropriate in the acute stage of pain but may be maintained thereafter by operant conditioning until its adaptive function is lost and it becomes maladaptive. It is perhaps useful to regard this as a subset of pain behaviour, as there are other forms of pain behaviour with obvious adaptive functions, such as appropriate help-seeking and compliance with therapeutic regimens. These behaviours are equally amenable to operant conditioning, and it makes little sense to leave them out of the reckoning. Unfortunately, however, the pejorative connotations of 'pain behaviour' have been handed on unchallenged; for example, Turk *et al.* (1985), in their empirical examination of the construct with health professionals, identified four clusters of pain behaviours on which there was agreement – distorted ambulation or posture, negative affect, facial/audible expressions of distress, and avoidance of activity. Vlaeyen *et al.* (1987) further characterized pain patients by three dimensions: withdrawal–approach, high arousal –low arousal and visible–audible, and suggested that treatment should be guided by where a patient was located in the schema: high-arousal types might be treated by relaxation training, for example, and high-approachers by operant conditioning aimed at abolishing excessive pain behaviours and shaping more adequate well behaviours. These approaches to assessment and treatment have been developed from consideration of the problems of chronic pain, but they are concerned solely with the identification and abolition of maladaptive patterns of behaviour; some make no attempt to investigate self-reported pain; some concentrate on classifying people as behavioural 'types'. As a contrast, the power of including a range of behaviours in pain assessment was demonstrated in Klein and Charlton's (1980) study of burn injury patients, in which it was shown that verbal 'well behaviours' outnumbered verbal complaints during very painful procedures. Although this work was carried out in an acute pain setting, its value was in identifying coping behaviour, which is of potentially great significance in persistent and chronic pain. This is not the story of penicillin; these therapeutic attributes are unlikely to be discovered unless they are sought actively.

The notion of assessing other pain behaviours such as coping skills, attributions and meaning has been gaining ground, but the literature on assessment still tends to be focused on maladaptive responses or expressions of suffering. While the assessment and monitoring of suffering behaviour is important in acute pain, a wider use of the term 'pain behaviour' to include adaptive responses and function is an asset in studies of both chronic and acute pain, especially in studies of therapeutic intervention.

Traditional models of scientific inquiry are based around the notions of quantification and categorization. Many methods of pain assessment assume that pain can be quantified in numerical units, like length or volume, and thus can be measured in a similar way. This approach allows comparisons between scores to be made, and permits statistical analysis of the data so generated, providing that the meaning (nominal, ordinal, interval, ratio) of the numbers is established. It is exemplified by laboratory studies on pain threshold and pain tolerance, which use standard stimuli and treat pain as a sensory experience like pressure or heat. Other approaches use categorical methodologies, based on pain descriptors or on patterns of disturbed function related to pain. Another approach is by physiological measures such as blood pressure or palmar sweat.

The concept of pain as a sensation was challenged by Melzack (1975: 278) when he wrote 'To describe pain solely in terms of intensity is like specifying the visual world only in terms of light flux without regard to pattern, colour, texture, and the many other dimensions of visual experience' and by Wall (1977: 363): 'I could simply sense a pure red light with the simplest unique perception and cognition to follow. I wish to submit that I have never sensed a pure pain in a similar fashion. If I sense a pain, it comes in a packet with such changes as fear, loathing, anxiety, dislike, urgency etc.' These words invite the notion of pain as perception rather than sensation, but they fall short of the 'multidimensional experience' described by R. Chapman (1984). Many pain measurement tools fall short in the same way by attempting to quantify pain using a single dimension of amount or severity. Crude and limited though they are, such tools are used widely and tend to demonstrate replicability and face validity. More sophisticated scales may also contain numerical estimates of amount of distressfulness and/or functional limitation. Categorical and functional measures may incorporate more 'real-life' factors such as meaning, coping style and disruptiveness, all of which impinge on and are impinged on by the pain experience.

The tools of assessment

Assessment and measurement tools and techniques may be divided roughly into three types: self-report scales, observational techniques and physiological measures. Research reports have demonstrated the wide variations in levels of sophistication within the three types, and between uni- and multidimensional approaches.

Self-report scales

Self-report scales range from simple visual analogue scales, numerical rating scales and verbal scales to more-or-less structured interviews or questionnaires incorporating variables such as coping skills, meaning, and functional limitation. Some examples are described below.

Visual analogue scales, verbal numerical scales and verbal descriptive scales

In its simplest form, the visual analogue scale (VAS) is a 10-centimetre horizontal line with indicators of severity such as 'no pain' at one end and 'worst pain possible' at the other. Indicators of other aspects of pain such as unpleasantness and impact on life have also been assessed by VAS. In the case of severity, the scalee is invited to make a single mark across the line corresponding to the level of pain. The scale is scored by measuring the distance from the 'no pain' end to the mark, usually in millimetres, giving the possibility of finely graded scoring from 0 to 100 points (or 1 to 101 depending on how the no pain end is pegged). Some studies have reported that scalees prefer the VAS to a 4 or 5-point verbal rating scale (VRS) (Joyce et al. 1975), but Jensen et al. (1994) report on others which have found a higher rate of failure for accurate completion (4–11 per cent) for VASs in comparison with other simple methods. Wilkie et al. (1990), however, have shown that failure rates are reduced significantly if the measure is fully explained to the scalee beforehand.

The discriminative functions of the VAS have been investigated by Jensen *et al.* (1994) who argued that 100/1 points may be too many for meaningful discrimination, and demonstrated that most people use multiples of 5 or 10 in rating pain, effectively reducing the 101 potential points to 11 or 21.

The status of the numerical scores derived from such scales has been demonstrated by Price *et al.* (1994), who have shown ratio scale properties for a simple VAS and a mechanical (slide-rule) version, the M-VAS, for separate measures of pain intensity and pain unpleasantness. They also demonstrated internal consistency for their VAS and M-VAS as measures of both experimental (concurrent) and clinical (remembered) pain, but argued that not all pain VASs are likely to be ratio scales; the measurement properties of the scales are influenced by three factors:

◆ the specific words used to anchor the end-points
◆ the length of the line
◆ the instructions as to how to use them.

Price *et al.* (1994) also showed that their 0–10 numerical rating scales of pain intensity and pain unpleasantness were internally consistent but lacked ratio scale properties.

The sensitivity and uniformity of distribution of scores on VASs in different orientations were investigated by Ogon *et al.* (1996) who assessed a group of chronic low back pain patients on horizontal and vertical visual analogue scales, and demonstrated higher sensitivity in the horizontal orientation for a scale of *usual pain intensity*.

Syrjala and Chapman (1984) have pointed out the ease with which VASs can be completed by sick patients or those with limited language capacity on the one hand, and the oversimplification of the experience of pain inherent in the method on the other. Although the use of multiple VASs targeting different aspects of pain may produce a richer account of the experience, the linearity of the judgements made on such scales, and the status of the numerical data derived should be demonstrated, as in Price *et al.*'s (1994) study, rather than assumed.

Verbal scales

A simple verbal scale (VS) of pain severity is derived from a VAS with the line divided by reference points such as mild pain, moderate pain, severe pain, in increasing order of magnitude, or presented as a list:

---

no pain   mild pain   moderate pain   severe pain   worst pain

no pain
mild pain
moderate pain
severe pain

It is common practice to assign numerical scores 0–3 or 4 to the items. However, equal intervals between the points cannot be assumed unless preliminary scaling has been carried out and the scale constructed only from those items with good agreement for scale position and numerical score across a large number of subjects. In the absence of these procedures, the assigned numbers may be assumed to represent a nominal scale only, which is a constraint on statistical analytic procedures. Moreover, 4 or 5 points on the scale gives too broad band-widths between points, which may result in over- or underestimation of treatment effects, as Jensen *et al.* (1994) have argued.

Littman *et al.* (1985) carried out a series of studies of response to analgesia, and assessed the relative performance of a VAS and verbal scales of pain intensity and pain relief at scheduled times after drug dosing. The VAS was a conventional 10-cm horizontal line with the 0 end designated 'no pain' and the 100 end 'worst pain I've ever felt'. The verbal intensity scale was rated at baseline as 0 (none), 1 (mild), 2 (moderate), 3 (severe), and in some cases 4 (very severe). The verbal relief scale was filled in relative to pain at the start of the study, and was pegged at 4 (complete), 3 (a lot), 2 (moderate), 1 (a little) and 0 (none). Littman *et al.* (1985) reported that the scales correlated strongly with one another, with minimal and inconsistent differences between them. Overall, the pain relief scale was somewhat more sensitive than the VAS, which in turn showed a small advantage over the verbal pain intensity rating. They concluded that the choice of scale might not be critical, except that the verbal pain intensity scale appeared to be less sensitive than the others, as other researchers have commented.

Questionnaires – descriptive

The McGill Pain Questionnaire (MPQ) (Melzack 1975) is basically a verbal descriptive scale, with the addition of an indicator of localization, questions about medication and previous pain, change in pain over time, and a verbal rating scale of Present Pain Intensity (PPI). The verbal descriptive scale is an attempt to capture estimates of both the intensity and the quality of the pain experience. It was constructed by giving 102 pain descriptors to a group of subjects who were asked to sort them into groups which described different aspects of pain. This preliminary sorting resulted in the identification of three major groups of words denoted *sensory*, *affective* and *evaluative*; for example:

sensory	*affective*	*evaluative*
flickering	punishing	annoying
quivering	gruelling	troublesome
pulsing	cruel	miserable
throbbing	vicious	intense
beating	killing	unbearable
pounding		

Some later studies have cast doubt upon the split between the affective and evaluative scales (e.g. Crockett *et al*. 1977; Byrne *et al*. 1982). Following the preliminary grouping, groups of doctors, patients and students were asked to assign an intensity value to each of the words. There was no overall agreement on the intensity values, but adequate overall agreement for the relative positions (rank ordering) of the words. This raises questions about the numerical status of the Pain Rating Index (PRI), which is the sum of the rank values of all the word sets, and the alternative score obtained by summing or averaging the word set scores on each scale. A simple count of the number of words chosen from each scale is also used in some studies. Several writers have expressed concern about the complexity and unusualness of some of the words (e.g. lancinating).

A further part of the MPQ is Present Pain Intensity, a 0–5-point verbal scale:

0 no pain
1 mild
2 discomforting
3 distressing
4 horrible
5 excruciating

These words were taken from a previously determined ordering of pain-evaluative words, and were chosen because they were 'approximately' equally far apart on mean rankings. As with the three scales, there are good grounds for accepting the rank ordering of the items, but equal interval scaling is not well established (one possible reason is that the intervals are simply not equal). Sensitivity is a potential problem with only five categories, but studies have shown close correlations with the evaluative score (Graham *et al*. 1980) and with a VAS pain intensity scale (Walsh and Leber 1983). The scale can be administered as a paper-and-pencil test or in interview format, and there is a short form (Melzack 1987).

Syrjala and Chapman (1984) commented on the growing number of studies which support the basic structure of the MPQ, its reliability and concurrent validity, but Holroyd *et al*. (1992), in a multicentre study of its use, claim that many of the studies have serious methodological problems, and question the value of the PRI in diagnosis or in identifying useful subgroups. They recommend that sensory subclass scores be retained for analysis and not combined into a single sensory dimension (although this information is unstandardized as yet).

Studies (e.g. Allen and Weinmann 1982; Melzack *et al*. 1986) have tended to confirm the idea of some typical patterns of responses for pain associated with different acute and chronic clinical syndromes such as headache and facial pain. Finally there is some evidence that the selective use of affective words is related to emotional disturbance in some patients. The predictive significance of this finding is not clear, but it is a potential problem in assessing pain in some psychiatric patients.

Scales which relate pain to functional limitation

Functional scales have been developed to meet a clinical need. Where the focus of clinical interest is on the reduction or elimination of disability related to pain, scales such as the Oswestry Low Back Pain Disability Questionnaire (Fairbank *et al.* 1980), the Clinical Back Pain questionnaire (Ruta *et al.* 1994) and the Pain Disability Index (Tait *et al.* 1990) are a structured way of exploring that relationship and monitoring change. Many of these scales are condition-specific, although the Pain Disability Index was developed and standardized on a mixed group of chronic pain patients. The measures vary widely in the extent to which scaling parameters have been considered in their construction. The Oswestry, for example, contains verbal/numerical rating scales with 6 or 10 points, some (functional) arranged vertically:

(　) pain does not prevent me walking any distance
(　) pain prevents me walking more than 1 mile
(　) pain prevents me walking more than $\frac{1}{2}$ mile
(　) pain prevents me walking more than $\frac{1}{4}$ mile
(　) I can only walk using a stick or crutches
(　) I am in bed most of the time and can only crawl to the toilet

and some (severity) arranged horizontally:

How severe do you think your problem is regarding your back pain?

1	2	3	4	5	6	7	8	9	10

not   major
                                                              incapacitating
                                                                      problem

and horizontal self-efficacy scales (from Nicholas 1989):

I can enjoy things, despite the pain

0	1	2	3	4	5	6

not at all   completely
confident   confident

The functional scales cover pain intensity, personal care, lifting, walking, sitting, standing, sleeping, sex life, social life and travelling. Each subscale consists of six items, which appears to be an arbitrary choice and which brings its sensitivity into question. Moreover, while the items have been arranged in an ordinal fashion, the size of the intervals between them has not been addressed and is unlikely to be equal.

In contrast, Ruta *et al.* (1994) addressed the issue of psychometric status in designing the Clinical Back Pain Questionnaire (CBPQ), which was based on questions asked during the clinical interview. The questions have different numbers of possible responses (between three and six) and are a mixture of Likert-type scales with ordinal scoring:

> In the last two weeks, for how many days did you suffer pain in the back or legs?
> None at all (0)
> Between 1 and 5 days (1)
> Between 6 and 10 days (2)
> For more than 10 days (3)

and categorical responses with multiple choices each given a score of 1 (scores were then summed):

> Is the pain made worse by any of the following?
> Coughing ( )
> Sneezing ( )
> Sitting ( )
> Standing ( )
> Bending ( )
> Walking ( )

The total score range is 0–100, and apart from at the extremes, an obvious problem is that the same score may be derived from a number of different configurations of subscores.

The questionnaire was pre-tested and piloted, and checked for factorial structure, internal consistency (between-item and item-total), test-retest reliability and construct validity against a standardized test – the SF-36, referral pattern, analgesic use and general practitioner's prediction of symptom severity. Total scores were shown to be normally distributed. An added refinement to the summative scoring would be to have a graphical representation of individual score patterns so that detail is not lost. That being said, the CBPQ represents a bridge between the needs of clinical assessment and research, in that it demonstrates that clinically relevant data may be collected with relative ease and with an eye to mulivariate analysis.

Tait *et al.* (1990) developed a brief index of pain-related disability, the Pain Disability Index (PDI), partly in response to the unwieldy lengths of other scales. The PDI consists of seven categories of activity, with responses to be entered on a numerical rating scale of 10 points arranged along a horizontal line, anchored at each end:

> 1   Family/home responsibilities
> This category refers to activities related to the home or family. It includes chores or duties performed around the house (e.g. yard work) and errands or favours for other family members (e.g. driving the children to school)

1	2	3	4	5	6	7	8	9	10
no disability									total disability

The PDI was shown to have good internal consistency, and concurrent valid-ity when compared with indices of pain behaviour, but not with other indices of disability such as time spent resting and work tolerance (although patients were on a highly structured work programme). Test-retest reliability was somewhat low, which may have had something to do with the arbitrary scoring – what do the numbers mean? Sensitivity is also lost by summing across domains.

These examples of attempts to measure functional disability reflect the problems inherent in the approach – what to measure, how to capture the essential parameters without unwieldiness, how to construct a scoring system which is not only statistically reliable and valid but sensitive and useful. See Kopec and Esdaile (1995) for a review of functional disability scales for back pain and comment on methodological issues.

Observational techniques

Observational methods include recording variables such as time spent rest-ing, medication use, sleep patterns and verbal/motor 'pain behaviour'. They tend to be costly in terms of time and the need for trained observers, but may be the preferred option in cases where self-report is felt to be unreli-able or not possible, as in the pain assessment of small children, people with severe learning disabilities, or those with other communication prob-lems. Studies have tended to show poor correlations between observational techniques and self-report measures (see for example Richards *et al.* 1982), suggesting the need for further investigations into the relationship between the two. The need for structured, reliable and valid observation measures, for inter-rater reliability to be established, and for observers to be trained and not just experienced is highlighted in studies such as that of Choiniere *et al.* (1990) in which observations were carried out by nurses during and immediately after burn injury patients had undergone painful procedures (debridement, dressing change). Nurses and patients rated *pain intensity* and *pain relief with analgesic medication*. The nurses frequently under- or over-estimated the pain experienced by the patients, when they were not only undergoing the procedures but also at rest. While less experienced nurses tended to overestimate pain during procedures, those who had worked on burns units for longer tended to underestimate. The degree of relief from analgesic medication was overestimated; patients reported inadequate relief and were often given low doses.

Keefe and Block (1982) demonstrated the usefulness of precisely defined behaviours and training for staff in a series of observational studies. They constructed operational behavioural definitions of certain behaviours iden-tified as commonly associated with pain, including guarded movement, bracing, grimacing and sighing. In the studies, trained observers rated the frequency of these behaviours in chronic low back pain patients undergoing a treatment programme. Among the findings were: a positive relationship between observer ratings and patient self-report, the reliability of the ratings, and a change in most of the behaviours between the intake and discharge ratings. A further refinement of the observational scaling technique was developed by Richards *et al.* (1982), who added well behaviours to their University of Alabama, Birmingham (UAB) Pain Behaviour Scale. However, correlation with self-report measures was weak pre-treatment and although it improved post-treatment, it failed to reach significance. Results such as these suggest that observational techniques in adult pain patients show some potential when trained observers are used and terms are precisely defined, but are not yet refined or developed enough to yield valid, reliable and useful results.

Physiological measures

The search for 'objectivity' in pain assessment has led some researchers to use measures of autonomic function or disease activity as analogues for the experience of pain. A correlation between joint inflammation and reported joint pain in rheumatoid arthritis, or reported back pain and heart rate or palmar sweating would be expected, for example. It is as if reported pain is unreliable but physical measures are not, or as if there is, after all, a close relationship between tissue damage and pain. Indices of autonomic function are notoriously difficult to capture and quantify, responding as they do to a variety of internal and external events, and given their tendency to fluctuate and fade even when conditions appear to be constant. Parameters such as joint inflammation measured by thermography and muscle tension measured by EMG (electromyogram) have also proved to be unreliable indicators of clinical pain. In the case of autonomic function, short-term changes in palmar sweating and heart-rate acceleration indicative of arousal/distress, have been reported in infants undergoing heel lancing, as might be expected with a sudden noxious stimulus, but in chronic pain, indications of arousal are usually absent or variable. Andrasik *et al.* (1982) and S.L. Chapman (1986) have reviewed studies of measures such as EMG, skin temperature, blood flow and skin resistance in headache and chronic muscle contraction respectively, and have reported inconsistent or contradictory findings. That these results may, in some cases, be due to methodological shortcomings should be borne in mind. S.L. Chapman (1986) has suggested that a longitudinal study of EMG and thermal parameters in a naturalistic setting needs to be undertaken in order to provide background and baseline data. Wolf *et al.* (1982) have demonstrated the need for EMG measures to be undertaken in both static and dynamic modes in order to increase the correspondence between the measures and pain report. Rather than attempting to measure physiological changes directly, McCracken *et al.* (1992) used self-report of characteristic physiological responses such as sweating, palpitations and dizziness/faintness in attempting to capture anxiety/fear of pain. Fear has been implicated in the maintenance of pain behaviour (fear of pain leads to avoidance of activity, which is maintained/ reinforced by fear reduction). Some of the difficulties inherent in measuring physiological concomitants of emotional states directly were circumvented by this method. The researchers constructed the Pain Anxiety Symptoms Scale (PASS) which samples three response modes: cognitive, overt behavioural and physiological. Sample physiological items include:

I become sweaty when in pain
Pain seems to cause my heart to pound or race
When I sense pain, I feel dizzy or faint
I have pressure or tightness in my chest when in pain

The scale was administered to 104 consecutive referrals to a multidisciplinary pain clinic. Internal reliability was demonstrated for the overall scale and the subscales, and validity was supported by significant correlations with measures of anxiety and disability. These reports of physiological symptoms represent gross changes; clearly, direct measures such as skin resistance are much more sensitive than self-reported sweating, but given the PASS's performance with a group of chronic pain patients and the problems of direct measurement, the PASS has been shown to be a useful instrument in assessing the fear of pain in three response modes.

Further consideration to the affective components of pain is given in Chapter 5 on personal, social and cultural factors. The matter of self-report versus 'objective' physical measures will be further considered in the section on measuring pain in children (pp. 102–6), where self-report may not be an option, and in the biofeedback section of Chapter 7 on interventions (pp. 118–22).

Assessing pain in children

The history of the assessment and treatment of pain in children is in some respects a sorry tale, with evidence of underestimation of pain levels and consequent undermedication in a number of hospital-based studies. Beyer *et al.* (1983) investigated analgesic use in clinical populations and found that children received around 30 per cent of the analgesics they were prescribed, while adults received around 70 per cent. The situation does not appear to have changed since then. Hester (1995) cites studies which suggest that over 50 per cent of children may experience post-operative pain needlessly, in spite of significant advances in pain management. Some of these findings may be related to fears about overdosing children: Finley *et al.* (1993) found that parents tended to give their children inadequate doses of prescribed analgesics after surgery, even when they knew their children were in pain. Other reasons may be to do with misunderstandings about children's pain behaviour. Hamers *et al.* (1996) showed that paediatric nurses attributed more pain to children who expressed their pain vocally than to those who expressed themselves less vocally or not at all. P.A. McGrath (1987), however, has pointed out that quiescence and withdrawal from activity is a characteristic response in some children and with certain types of pain. Eland and Andersen (1977) suggested that one of the myths about pain in children is that because they do not exhibit pain behaviour in the same way that adults do, they do not feel pain in the same way and therefore require less pain control. Other myths include the idea that children recover quickly and suffer no long-term effects from episodes of pain, and that there is a danger of addiction if they are administered narcotic medication. Thompson and Varni (1986) have pointed out that there is little evidence to support these assumptions. Indeed, P.J. McGrath (1995) has reviewed studies showing robust age-related findings on response to and understanding of pain in clinical settings. One suggestion is that because children under 5 have difficulty in understanding that pain associated with needles will be over quickly, and they cannot easily learn to use new, adaptive coping strategies, they experience *more* pain than older children. P.J. McGrath and McAlpine (1993) have documented a developmental sequence of children's understanding of pain, which draws on evidence of anticipatory fear of pain at 6 months, and sophisticated avoidance behaviour by 18 months. Ericksson (1990) has commented on the potential interrelationships between variables such as anxiety, loneliness and expectations about treatment, and pain. The role of factors such as context, cultural background, family influences and early learning experiences are only now beginning to be explored systematically (P.J. McGrath 1987).

The accurate assessment of pain in children is necessary for diagnosis, adequate pain management, determination of the most appropriate method of pain relief, and monitoring the continuing effectiveness of interventions (Ericksson 1990). The need for this accuracy has become more urgent in recent times, as the outcome of many severe illnesses in children has improved greatly, often at the expense of long and painful treatments. Furthermore, the impact of early stresses such as pain on later physical and mental health is beginning to be elucidated (see Stevenson 1995). There has been a consequent interest in and proliferation of assessment tools.

As P.A. McGrath (1987) has pointed out, the criteria for a valid and useful measure of pain in children are largely the same as those for measures in adults: reliability, specificity, bias-freeness, versatility (for assessing different types of pain) and applicability in a variety of situations. A special problem in assessing children is the influence of developmental level, which will determine not only verbal ability and skill with a pen or pencil, but gross motor behaviour and cognitive attributes such as concepts of amount and number, the use of symbol and metaphor in communication, and the ability to comprehend a scale of any kind as referring to oneself.

Hamilton and Zeltzer (1995), P.J. McGrath and Unruh (1990) and P.A. McGrath (1987) have also commented on the importance of the pain context, parental attitudes and behaviour, and previous pain experience of the child, in children's response to pain. The context might include the clinic room and nurse in a mask and gown as signals that a painful procedure was about to take place, as in burns dressing changes. Studies have shown that children do not habituate to this procedure; they respond to the cues that it is about to take place with distressed behaviour which may make any additional behaviours due to pain hard to discriminate. Parental attitudes and behaviour may also act as cues for distress around pain or painful procedures.

There is evidence that previous painful experiences act as markers against which new pains are judged; in a study by Lollar *et al.* (1982) children with little previous pain experience tended to overestimate the intensity of 'the most hurt' they had experienced compared to children who had experienced some previous pain. On the other hand, Hamilton and Zeltzer (1995) have pointed out that previous distressing pain situations and unsuccessful coping attempts may lead to anticipatory anxiety, decreased self-confidence and negative expectations for handling future pain-producing events. Pain and anxiety are so interrelated and so hard to distinguish in either behavioural or physiological terms that some researchers (e.g. Katz *et al.* 1980) have advocated the use of the term 'distress' to cover both. Studies such as those by Kavanagh (1983) and Lasoff and McEttrick (1986) on burn pain in children have shown that when the anxiety component of the distress is reduced, indicators of pain (such as medication needs) are also reduced. The studies were an attempt to minimize the unpredictable and uncontrollable aspects of burns dressing changes in children by giving one group fore-knowledge of the procedure and allowing them to help remove bandages, apply cream and even help with debridement. In addition, the nurse wore a piece of red tape on her apron during the procedure, and removed it when things were 'safe'. Another group of children received standard care. The experimental group needed less pain medication between dressing changes, and demonstrated better physical and psychological outcomes which were evident at follow-up after discharge. Results such as these highlight the interdependence of pain and anxiety and the need for assessment procedures to take this into account also.

Physiological measures

In infants, reactions to noxious procedures such as heel lancing have been assessed by physiological measures such as heart-rate acceleration, respiratory responses and palmar sweating. Hester (1995) has pointed out that reliance on physiological measures alone is risky; they have been shown to be sensitive to pain but not specific for pain. P.A. McGrath (1987) has commented on the need for research into infants' physiological responses to novel or stressful non-noxious events in order to determine which responses may be specific to pain. In older children, it has been equally difficult to determine whether physiological indices of physical stress or distress are measures of pain or of anxiety related to noxious procedures. There is as yet no known non-invasive test for a pain-specific physiological reaction. Hester (1995) reports on work (as yet unpublished) which uses an observational technique to capture changes of physiological origin, such as respiratory patterns and effort; skin colour, texture and moistness, and brightness of eyes. Early reports of internal consistency and inter-rater reliability are promising; validity and specificity for pain have yet to be determined.

Behavioural measures

Studies of behavioural responses to noxious stimuli in infants have included crying, body movements, rigidity and facial expression. Examples of behaviour observation tools include the Burns Treatment Distress Scale (BTDS) (Elliott and Olson 1983), the Neonatal Facial Coding System (Grunau and Craig 1990), and the Children's Hospital of Eastern Ontario Pain Scale (CHEOPS) (P.A. McGrath *et al.* 1985) for post-operative pain. There are individual and developmental differences in body movement and rigidity, and initial state of alertness affects patterns of crying and facial expression (Grunau and Craig 1987), suggesting that the baseline arousal state may be important in nociception and/or pain behaviour. In older children there are age-specific patterns of responses, but as Hester (1995) has pointed out, it is difficult to know if behaviours are responses to pain or the child's way of preventing or coping with pain. Further, motor/verbal behaviour may be blunted as a response to pain, as well as enhanced, and few tests are designed to capture this important variation. An exception is the Child Pain Scale (Gauvain-Picquard *et al.* 1987) for cancer pain. Finally, both Hester and McGrath have pointed out the necessity of plotting behavioural scores over time and events in order to give a clearer picture of characteristic patterns of pain response in children.

Self-report measures

The youngest age at which children can give reliable reports of their pain is not an absolute, as there is quite wide variation in the ages at which cognitive developmental stages are attained in young children. Mathews *et al.* (1993) have suggested that 4 years is the youngest age at which self-report can be attempted. However, basic levels of verbal comprehension, linguistic skill and paper-and-pencil competence need to be ascertained before such techniques are applied. Carter (1994) has pointed out that illness and hospitalization may create a degree of regression.

There is a plethora of self-report tools for assessing pain in children; most of them concentrate on the single dimension of intensity. Some have been developed to elicit scalable responses by children too young to manage verbal or numerical scales (from 3–4 years old). Examples are the

Wong and Baker Faces Rating Scale (1988) and Oucher Scale (Beyer *et al.* 1992) on which responses are made by pointing to pictures of graded 'pain faces', and the Hester Poker Chip Tool (Hester *et al.* 1990) in which children choose a number of chips (from 1 to 4) to indicate amount of pain. Although these tools have been shown to be acceptable and usable to children, there are serious doubts about sensitivity, the numerical scores associated with the faces (especially the Oucher), whether they are measuring pain or distress, and about the conflation of number and amount on the Poker Chip Tool. Bieri *et al.* (1990) developed a faces scale with seven choices, pegged at the zero end with a neutral face, and with apparent ratio scaling properties; P.J. McGrath *et al.* (1985) showed internal consistency in children over 5 on a 9-point faces scale, with the numerical scores derived from the children's assessment of *affective magnitude*.

Traditional visual analogue 10-cm line scales have also been used as pain measures in children, in both horizontal and vertical orientations. They may be regarded as the next step up from pointing to faces in terms of language skills and vocabulary. In adults, the horizontal orientation was shown to be more sensitive and uniform with respect to score distribution (Ogon *et al.* 1996), and Price *et al.* (1994) have argued that the length of the line, the instructions and end-point descriptors have a strong influence on the sensitivity and scaling properties of the tool.

Simple descriptive and numerical scales have been used with children from 5 years old. While some studies have found them reliable, they have the same problems of sensitivity and numerical meaning as when used with adults.

The use of colours to denote intensity of pain has been used by researchers such as Eland (1989) and Stewart (1977), but Hester *et al.* (1992) have pointed out the lack of convergence between colour choice and intensity ratings. It is likely that factors such as affect and a preference for red are also a factor in colour choice.

More comprehensive assessments include the Pediatric Pain Questionnaire (Tesler *et al.* 1983) developed with children 9–12 with a range of painful conditions, and the Varni/Thompson Pediatric Pain Questionnaire (1987), which child, parent and physician fill in; there are child and adolescent versions, the age range covering 4–19 years and experiencing chronic pain. These scales acknowledge the multidimensional nature of the pain experience, and variously contain assessments of sensation, expectation, coping skills, pain vocabulary, pain-related affect, location, knowledge and concepts about pain.

Conclusion

Pain, with all its complexities, has proved elusive as an entity to be assessed or measured, partly because adequate descriptive and explanatory models are still in development; partly because it is inherently difficult to capture the salient parameters of a multifaceted subjective experience, and partly because the arbitrary assignment of crude numerical values to measures such as intensity has produced scales deficient in sensitivity. Currently, a large number of different types of scales exist; few are good predictors of outcome. Self-report assessments for both acute and chronic pain range from simple sensory unimodal scales such as the VAS, through more complex verbal scales such as the McGill PQ, with its attempt to capture evaluative and emotional aspects of pain, to the structured clinical interview embodied in the CBPQ with its focus on function. Some scales concentrate on the pain itself, and some on its effects and concomitants. Observational techniques may be the tools of choice when self-report is impossible or unreliable, but they need precise behavioural definitions of items and trained observers if subjective bias is to be avoided. Physiological techniques have the theoretical advantage of objectivity, but are difficult to administer and tend to be insensitive and unreliable except in reflecting short-term reactions to noxious stimuli. Scales borrowed from other domains, such as the MMPI from Psychiatry, have yet to demonstrate their usefulness convincingly, although they go on being used. The assessment of pain in children, who may be preliterate or have limited vocabularies, is potentially even more challenging than that in adults, yet the problems associated with the tools are very similar. There are quick, bedside scales suitable for use in acute (often procedural) pain, which tend to be unidimensional and to have questionable scalability and sensitivity; at the other end of the spectrum are developmentally appropriate tools, which often, although not always, lack numerical rigour. A major problem in assessing pain in children is the question of what is being measured; pain, distress, or a combination of the two. More comprehensive tools, such as the Multidimensional Pain Questionnaire described by P.J. McGrath (1987) contain both quantitative and qualitative elements and give a richer picture which has also proved to be reliable and valid. It may be that although such tools would be regarded as too cumbersome and lengthy to be useful in assessing acute and procedural pain, they could be used on intake whenever pain is to be expected, to give a baseline. Such tools could also be designed so as to incorporate valid, reliable and sensitive individual components suitable for acute pain assessment. This approach could be invaluable in adult pain assessment too. The need, in assessing pain in both children and adults, is not for more and more scales, but for more thoughtfully designed scales.

References

Allen, R.A. and Weinmann, R.L. (1982) The McGill Pain Questionnaire in the diagnosis of headache. *Headache*, 22: 20–9.

Andrasik, F., Blanchard, E.B., Arena, J.G., Saunders, N.L. and Barron, K.D. (1982) Psychophysiology of recurrent headache: methodological issues and new empirical findings. *Behaviour Therapy*, 13: 407–29.

Bates, M.S. (1987) Ethnicity and pain: a biocultural model. *Social Science and Medicine*, 24: 47–50.

Beyer, J.E., DeGood, D.E., Ashley, L.C. and Russell, G.A. (1983) Patterns of postoperative analgesic use with adults and children following cardiac surgery. *Pain*, 17: 71–81.

Beyer, J.E., Denyes, M.J. and Villaruel, A.M. (1992) The creation, validation and continuing development of the oucher: a measure of pain intensity in children. *Journal of Pediatric Nursing*, 7: 335–46.

Bieri, D., Reeve, R.A., Campion, G.D., Addicoat, L. and Ziegler, J.B. (1990) The faces pain scale for self-assessment of pain experienced by children: development, initial validation, and preliminary investigation for ratio scale properties. *Pain*, 41: 139–50.

Block, A.R. (1991) An additional perspective on the Fordyce/Schmidt controversy. *Pain*, 46: 234.

Byrne, M., Troy, A., Bradley, L.A., Marchisello, P.J., Geisinger, K.F., Van der Heide, L.H. and Prieto, E.J. (1982) Cross-validation of the factor structure of the McGill Pain Questionnaire. *Pain*, 13: 193–201.

Carter, B. (1994) Assessment and nature of pain, in *Child and Infant Pain: Principles of Nursing Care and Management*. London: Chapman and Hall.

Chapman, R. (1984) New directions in the understanding and management of pain. *Social Science and Medicine*, 19: 1261–77.

Chapman, S.L. (1986) A review and clinical perspective on the use of EMG and thermal biofeedback for chronic headaches. *Pain*, 27: 1–43.

Choiniere, M., Melzack, R., Girard, N., Rondeau, J. and Paquin, M. (1990) Comparisons between patients' and nurses' assessment of pain and medication efficacy in severe burn injuries. *Pain*, 40: 143–52.

Crockett, D.J., Prkachin, K.M. and Craig, K.D. (1977) Factors of the language of pain in patient and volunteer groups. *Pain*, 4: 175–82.

Eland, J.M. (1989) The effectiveness of transcutaneous electrical nerve stimulation (TENS) with children experiencing cancer pain, in S.G. Funk, E.M. Tornquist, M.T. Champagne, *et al.* (eds) *Key Aspects of Comfort: Management of Pain, Fatigue and Nausea*. New York: Springer.

Eland, J.M. and Andersen, J.E. (1977) The experience of pain in children, in A.K. Jacox (ed.) *Pain: A Source Book for Nurses and Other Health Professionals*. Boston, MA: Little, Brown.

Elliott, C.H. and Olson, R.A. (1983) The management of children's distress in response to painful medical treatments for burn injuries. *Behaviour Research and Therapy*, 21: 675–83.

Ericksson, C.J. (1990) Pain measurement in children: problems and directions. *Journal of Developmental and Behavioural Paediatrics*, 11: 135–7.

Fairbank, C.T., Davies, J.B., Couper, J.C. and O'Brien, J.P. (1980) The Oswestry Low Back Pain Disability Questionnaire. *Physiotherapy*, 66: 271–3.

Finley, G.A., McGrath, P.J., McNeill, G., Forward, P. and Fitzgerald, P. (1993) *Severity and Parents' Management of Postoperative Pain in Children*. IASP (International Association for the Study of Pain) Abstract book, 7th World Congress on Pain, Paris.

Fordyce, W.E. (1984) Behavioural science and chronic pain. *Postgraduate Medical Journal*, 60: 865–8.

Fordyce, W.E., Roberts, A.H. and Sternbach, R. (1985) The behavioural management of chronic pain: a response to critics. *Pain*, 22: 113–25.

Gauvain-Picquard, A., Rodary, C., Rezvani, A. and Lemerle, J. (1987) Pain in children aged 2–6 years: a new observational rating scale elaborated in a pediatric oncology unit – preliminary report. *Pain*, 31: 177–88.

Graham, C., Bond, S.S., Gerkovich, M.M. and Cook, M.R. (1980) Use of the McGill Pain questionnaire in the assessment of cancer pain: replicability and consistency. *Pain*, 8: 377–87.

Greenwald, H.P. (1991) Interethnic differences in pain perception. *Pain*, 44: 157–63.

Grunau, R.V.E. and Craig, K.D. (1987) Pain expression in neonates: facial action and cry. *Pain*, 28: 395–410.

Grunau, R.V.E. and Craig, K.D. (1990) Facial activity as a measure of neonatal pain expression, in D.C. Tyler and E.J. Krane (eds) *Advances in Pain Research and Therapy 15: Pediatric Pain*. New York: Raven Press.

Hamers, J.P.H., Abu-Saad, H.H., van den Hout, M.A., Halfens, R.J.G. and Kester, A.D.M. (1996) The influence of children's vocal expressions, age, medical diagnosis and information obtained from parents on nurses' pain assessments and decisions regarding interventions. *Pain*, 65: 53–61.

Hamilton, A. and Zeltzer, L. (1995) Psychological approaches to procedural pain. *Bailliere's Clinical Paediatrics*, 3: 601–17.

Hester, N.O. (1995) Assessment of acute pain, in A. Aynsley-Green, M.P. Ward-Platt and A.R. Lloyd-Thomas (eds) Stress and pain in infancy and childhood. *Bailliere's Clinical Paediatrics*, 3: 561–99.

Hester, N.O., Foster, R.L. and Kristensen, K. (1990) Measurement of pain in children: generalizability and validity of the Pain Ladder and Poker Chip tool, in D.C. Tyler and J. Krane (eds) *Advances in Pain Research and Therapy 15: Pediatric Pain*. New York: Raven Press.

Hester, N.O., Foster, R.L. and Beyer, J.E. (1992) Clinical judgement in assessing children's pain, in J.H. Watson and M.I. Donovan (eds) *Pain Management: Nursing Perspective*. St Louis, MO: Mosby-Yearbook.

Holroyd, K.A., Holm, J.E., Keefe, F.J. Turner, J.A. Bradley, L.A., Murphy, W.D., Johnson, P., Anderson, K., Hunkle, A.L. and O'Malley, W.B. (1992) A multicentre evaluation of the McGill Pain Questionnaire: results from more than 1700 chronic pain patients. *Pain*, 41: 151–9.

Jensen, M.P., Karoly, P. and Harris, P. (1991) Assessing the affective component of chronic pain: development of the Pain Discomfort Scale. *Journal of Psychosomatic Research*, 35: 149–54.

Jensen, M.P., Turner, J.A. and Romano, J.M. (1994) What is the maximum number of levels needed in pain intensity measurement? *Pain*, 58: 387–92.

Joyce, C.R.B., Zutish, D.W., Hrubes, V. and Mason, R.M. (1975) Comparison of fixed interval and visual analogue scales for rating chronic pain. *European Journal of Clinical Pharmacology*, 18: 415–20.

Karoly, P. (1985) The assessment of pain: concepts and procedures, in P. Karoly (ed.) *Measurement Strategies in Health Psychology*. New York: John Wiley.

Katz, E.R., Kellerman, J. and Siegel, S.E. (1980) Behavioural distress in children with cancer undergoing painful medical procedures: developmental considerations. *Journal of Consulting and Clinical Psychology*, 48: 356–65.

Kavanagh, C. (1983) Psychological intervention with the severely burned child: report of an experimental comparison of two approaches and their effect on psychological sequelae. *Journal of the American Academy of Child Psychiatry*, 2: 145–56.

Keefe, F.J. and Block, A.R. (1982) Development of an observation method for assessing pain behaviour in chronic low back pain patients. *Behaviour Therapy*, 13: 363–75.

Keefe, F.J. and Williams, D.A. (1989) New directions in pain assessment and treatment. *Clinical Psychology Review*, 9: 549–68.

Klein, R.M. and Charlton, J.E. (1980) Behavioural observation and analysis of pain behaviour in critically burned patients. *Pain*, 9: 27–40.

Koopman, S., Eisenthal, S. and Stoeckle, J. (1984) Ethnicity in the reported pain, emotional distress and requests of medical patients. *Social Science and Medicine*, 18: 487–90.

Kopec, J.A. and Esdaile, J.M. (1995) Functional disability scales for back pain. *Spine*, 20: 1943–9.

Lasoff, E.M. and McEttrick, M.A. (1986) Participation versus distraction during dressing changes: can nurses' attitudes change? *Issues in Comprehensive Pediatric Nursing*, 9: 391–8.

Lipton, J.A. and Marbach, J.J. (1984) Ethnicity and the pain experience. *Social Science and Medicine*, 19: 1279–98.

Littman, G.S., Walker, B.R. and Schneider, B.E. (1985) Reassessment of verbal and visual analog ratings in analgesic studies. *Clinical Pharmacology and Therapeutics*, 38: 16–23.

Lollar, P.J., Smits, S.J. and Patterson, D.L. (1982) Assessment of paediatric pain: an empirical perspective. *Journal of Pediatric Psychology*, 7: 267–77.

Love, A. and Peck, C.L. (1987) The MMPI and psychological factors in chronic low back pain: a review. *Pain*, 28: 1–12.

McCracken, L.M., Zayfert, C. and Gross, R.T. (1992) The Pain Anxiety Symptoms Scale: development and validation of a scale to measure fear of pain. *Pain*, 50: 67–73.

McGrath, P.A. (1987) The multidimensional assessment and management of recurrent pain syndromes in children. *Journal of Behaviour Research and Therapy*, 25: 251–62.

McGrath, P.A., DeVeber, L.L. and Hearn, M.T. (1985) Multidimensional pain assessment in children, in H.L. Fields, R. Dubner and F. Cervero (eds) *Advances in Pain Research and Therapy 9*, Proceedings 4th World Congress on Pain. New York: Raven Press.

McGrath, P.J. (1987) Assessment of children's pain: a review of behavioural, physiological and direct scaling techniques. *Pain*, 31: 147–76.

McGrath, P.J. (1995) Aspects of pain in children and adolescents. *Journal of Child Psychology and Psychiatry*, 36: 717–30.

McGrath, P.J. and McAlpine, L.M. (1993) Psychological perspectives on children's pain. *Journal of Paediatrics*, 122: S2–S8.

McGrath, P.J. and Unruh, A.M. (1987) *Pain Research and Clinical Management, vol. 1: Pain in Children and Adolescents.* Amsterdam: Elsevier.

McGrath, P.J. and Unruh, A.M. (1990) Psychological treatment of pain in children and adolescents, in N. Schechter, C. Berde and M. Yaster (eds) *Pain in Infants, Children and Adolescents.* Baltimore, MD: Williams and Wilkins.

McGrath, P.J., Johnson, G., Goodman, J.T., Schillinger, J., Dunn, J. and Chapman, J. (1985) CHEOPS: a behavioural scale for rating post-operative pain in children. *Advances in Pain Research and Therapy*, 9: 395–402.

Mathews, J.R., McGrath, P.J. and Pigeon, H. (1993) Assessment and measurement of pain in children, in N. Schechter, C. Berde and M. Yaster (eds) *Pain in Infants, Children and Adolescents.* Baltimore, MD: Williams and Wilkins.

Melzack, R. (1975) The McGill Pain Questionnaire: major properties and scoring methods. *Pain*, 1: 277–99.

Melzack, R. (1987) The short-form McGill Pain Questionnaire. *Pain*, 30: 191–7.

Melzack, R. and Wall, P.D. (1982) *The Challenge of Pain*. Harmondsworth: Penguin.

Melzack, R., Terrence, C., Fromm, G. and Amsel, R. (1986) Trigeminal neuralgia and atypical facial pain: use of the McGill Pain questionnaire for discrimination and diagnosis. *Pain*, 27: 297–302.

Nicholas, M.K. (1989) Self-efficacy and chronic pain. Proceedings of the Annual Conference of the British Psychological Society, St Andrews, Scotland.

Ogon, M., Krismer, M., Sollner, W., Kantner-Rumplmair, W. and Lampe, A. (1996) Chronic low back pain measurement with visual analogue scales in different settings. *Pain*, 64: 425–8.

Price, D.D., Bush, F.M., Long, S. and Harkins, S.W. (1994) A comparison of pain measurement characteristics of mechanical visual analogue and simple numerical rating scales. *Pain*, 56: 217–26.

Richards, J.S., Nepomuceno, C., Riles, M. and Suer, Z. (1982) Assessing pain behaviour: the UAB Pain Behaviour Scale. *Pain*, 14: 393–8.

Roth, E., Davidoff, G., Haughton, J. *et al.* (1990) Functional assessment in spinal cord injury: a comparison of the modified Barthel Index and the 'adapted' Functional Independence Measure. *Clinical Rehabilitation*, 4: 277–85.

Ruta, D.A., Garratt, A.M., Wardlaw, D. and Russell, I.T. (1994) Developing a valid and reliable measure of health outcome for patients with low back pain. *Spine*, 19: 1887–96.

Schmidt, A.J.M. (1991) Reply to AR Block. *Pain*, 46: 235.

Stevenson, J. (1995) Long-term sequelae of acute stress in early life, in A. Aynsley-Green, M.P. Ward-Platt and A.R. Lloyd-Thomas (eds) Stress and pain in infancy and childhood. *Bailliere's Clinical Paediatrics*, 3: 619–31.

Stewart, M.L. (1977) Measurement of clinical pain, in J.K. Jacox (ed.) *Pain: A Source Book for Nurses and Other Health Professionals*. Boston, MA: Little, Brown.

Syrjala, K.L. and Chapman, C.R. (1984) Measurement of clinical pain: a review and integration of research findings. *Advances in Pain Research and Therapy*, 7: 71–101.

Tait, R.C., Chibnall, J.T. and Krause, S. (1990) The Pain Disability Index: psychometric properties. *Pain*, 40: 171–82.

Tesler, M., Ward, J. and Savedra, M. (1983) Developing an instrument for eliciting children's description of pain. *Perceptual and Motor Skills*, 56: 315–21.

Thompson, K.L. and Varni, S.W. (1986) A developmental, cognitive–behavioural approach to paediatric pain assessment. *Pain*, 31: 147–76.

Turk, D.C., Wack, J.T. and Kerns, R.D. (1985) An empirical examination of the 'pain-behaviour' construct. *Journal of Behavioural Medicine*, 8: 119–30.

Varni, S.W., Thompson, K.L. and Hanson, V. (1987) The Varni/Thompson Paediatric Pain Questionnaire 1. Chronic musculoskeletal pain in juvenile rheumatoid arthritis. *Pain*, 28: 27–38.

Vlaeyen, J.W.S., Van Eek, H., Groenman, N.H. and Schuerman, J.A. (1987) Dimensions and components of observed chronic pain behaviour. *Pain*, 31: 65–75.

Wall, P.D. (1977) Why do we not understand pain?, in R. Duncan and M. Weston-Smith (eds) *The Encyclopaedia of Ignorance, vol 2*. Oxford: Pergamon Press.

Wall, P.D. (1979) On the relation of injury to pain: the John J Bonica Lecture. *Pain*, 6: 253–64.

Walsh, T.D. and Leber, B. (1983) Measurement of chronic pain: visual analog scales and McGill Melzack Pain Questionnaire compared, in J.J. Bonica, U. Lindblom and A. Iggo (eds) *Advances in Pain Research and Therapy 5*. New York: Raven Press.

Wilkie, D.J., Holzemer, W.L. and Tesler, M.D. (1990) Measuring pain quality: validity and reliability of children and adolescents' pain language. *Pain*, 41: 151–9.

Williams, D.A. and Keefe, F.J. (1991) Pain beliefs and the use of cognitive behaviour strategies. *Pain*, 46: 185–90.

Winsberg, B. and Greenlick, M. (1975) Pain response in negro and white obstetrical patients, in M. Weisenberg (ed.) *Pain: Clinical and Experimental Perspectives*. St Louis, MO: C.V. Mosby.

Wolf, S.L., Nacht, M. and Kelly, J.L. (1982) EMG feedback training during dynamic movement for low back pain patients. *Behaviour Therapy*, 13: 395–406.

Wong, D.L. and Baker, C.M. (1988) *Reference Manual for the Wong–Baker Faces Pain Rating Scale*. Oklahoma City, OK: Wong and Baker Associates.

Interventions

The deliberate use of psychologic techniques for the
treatment of pain has a long past but a short history
(Sternbach 1984: 251)

Summary

In this chapter, psychological methods of management in acute and chronic
pain are reviewed. These include relaxation techniques, hypnosis, biofeedback, behavioural techniques and cognitive-behaviour therapy. Studies of
psychoanalytical psychotherapies for pain are virtually unknown except as
descriptive accounts of single cases, and these are not included. Each section
begins with an account of a treatment method and its clinical applications,
and also considers research findings.

Introduction

The very early history of psychological intervention for pain is not known,
but it is likely that simple techniques like distraction have been used inform-
ally in acute pain for centuries, and healers in many shapes and forms used
hypnosis-induced analgesia long before modern pharmacological techniques
were developed. Since the 1930s, behavioural science and clinical practice
have combined in a variety of techniques to alleviate and manage pain. The
work of researchers such as Jacobson (1938) demonstrated the efficacy of
progressive muscular relaxation in a range of disorders, including those
involving an element of pain. In the 1960s, Neal Miller and his associates
showed that autonomic nervous system functions could be modified by
operant conditioning, and thus provided the basis for one modern technique used in pain control: biofeedback (Miller 1974). Fordyce, in proposing and demonstrating the role of operant conditioning in chronic pain,
provided another (Fordyce 1984). Melzack and Wall's (1982) gate control
theory, which integrated neurophysiological and psychological factors in

pain perception, Wall's (1979) conceptualization of pain as an awareness of a need state, and cognitive-behavioural models proposed by writers such as Turk *et al.* (1983) also opened the way for the application of psychological models in pain management and treatment.

It may be said that psychological interventions for pain first earned their credentials by demonstrating the efficacy of behavioural methods in patients with hitherto intractable chronic pain. These patients were often referred to psychologists as a last resort, because they were thought to be neurotic or suffering from 'psychogenic' pain when physical treatment after treatment failed, and/or physical tests and examinations failed to discover an organic cause for their pain. Latterly, it has been recognized that whether or not pain can be shown to be organic in origin, it may be modified by psychological factors, and so treatment and management methods derived from psychological models have been extended to acute pain states such as those associated with medical procedures, surgery and oncology. An early and widely used technique, or set of techniques, is derived from Jacobson's (1938) work on progressive muscular relaxation.

Relaxation techniques

Early workers on relaxation techniques as therapeutic tools thought that there were two direct, simple reasons why relaxation techniques might be effective as treatments for pain: first, the pain is associated with muscular tension, and second, stress and anxiety are factors in the onset and maintenance of pain, and muscular relaxation is incompatible with stress/anxiety.

Relaxation training as a therapeutic technique was pioneered by Jacobson in the late 1930s, and developed by workers such as Benson (1975). Jacobson's (1938) method was predicated on the idea that muscular relaxation was a response incompatible with stress, and that training people to reduce muscular tension was an effective way to treat a wide variety of medical problems in which stress was implicated. Jacobson believed that relaxation of skeletal muscles was sufficient in itself to produce a positive therapeutic effect, and he taught his patients to relax muscle groups progressively, one by one, until they could achieve and sustain significant reductions in muscle tone all over their bodies. It was a lengthy process; typically Jacobson's subjects were taught to relax 44 different muscle groups in turn, and could take up to an hour to relax each one. In a series of studies, Jacobson demonstrated that in untrained subjects, tension remains high for a time after muscle contraction, even when the subject is instructed to relax, but his trained subjects could abolish residual tension almost immediately. Jacobson's technique was reported to be effective across a range of problems. He was careful to avoid using any kind of suggestion with his patients; he frequently went out of the room between sets of instructions so that he did not inadvertently influence the process.

Lehrer (1982) evaluated the technique and argued that it produces faster deeper and longer-lasting levels of muscular relaxation than later variations, which were much briefer. Curiously, in a study comparing Jacobson's with others, Lehrer comments that Jacobson's produced significantly lower self-reports of anxiety, but changes in measures of physiological arousal such as heart rate were not significantly different between the groups. Benson (1975) and his co-workers used a similar technique but considerably shortened it by instructing their patients to relax groups of muscles. There was an expectation of quiet, focused attention on the task of relaxation, but no other mentalistic phenomena were invoked.

The numerous later modifications of relaxation training typically take from 20 to 40 minutes to relax skeletal muscle groups, use tapes of instructions to aid within-treatment practice, and include some sort of calming mental exercise after the muscular relaxation. In some regimes, a period of controlled breathing is an added feature. Other variants, designed to have specific therapeutic effects such as pain control, often involve additional visual imagery instructions or positive self-talk. The common elements of all relaxation procedures are a quiet environment, a comfortable posture (often on a bed or couch), and progressive relaxation of skeletal muscles. In some regimes a predetermined order of muscle relaxation is used (to facilitate learning). In others, such as Autogenic Training, or Transcendental Meditation (TM) and other meditative techniques, no specific muscle-relaxing instructions are given but there is an expectation of muscle relaxation as the mental relaxation proceeds. Mental relaxation or quieting is achieved through the inner repetition of a mantra in TM, or through visual imagery or quiet concentration on parts of the body in others.

Although techniques such as Jacobson's began with increased muscle tension followed by relaxation, this is not appropriate for people with some painful conditions such as arthritis. A variation on the technique is for relaxation to proceed without initial muscle tensing. In autogenic training relaxation is produced by attention to breathing ('breathing in feelings of relaxation, breathing out tension and pain') accompanied by the inner repetition of suggestions of progressive looseness, heaviness and warmth all over the body (Luthe and Schultz 1969).

Relaxation training is now very widely used in numerous variations for many different types of condition, often in combination with other therapies. Studies of its effect on pain have included its use with tension headache, migraine, low back pain and rheumatoid arthritis. Turk et al. (1979) review a number of studies in which relaxation has been used as a 'control' condition for biofeedback conditioning in pain; Solbach et al. (1984) compared it with EMG and Thermal feedback in menstrual migraine; McCauley et al. (1983) compared relaxation and hypnosis for the treatment of chronic low back pain. Typically, relaxation has been shown to be an effective treatment for pain. In many studies it has proved to be as effective as more complex or expensive forms of treatment, or those requiring highly trained practitioners, such as biofeedback and hypnosis. Controlled studies of relaxation alone are virtually unknown because of the difficulty of providing a suitable control condition.

A major problem with the evaluation of relaxation therapy, apart from the difficulties of subject selection, adequate controls, and baseline measures, has been to isolate a specific effect or set of effects. Successful relaxation is associated with decreased autonomic arousal and decreased skeletal muscle tension, which may have direct effects on pain by decreasing tension in skeletal muscles and increasing peripheral blood flow, and indirect effects by reducing arousal. Because it involves quiet focused attention to the instructions, it may also act as a distractor. Further, it is essentially a self-management technique, with implications for mastery and thereby raised self-efficacy, which have also been shown to have an impact on pain.

Linton (1982) has reviewed twenty-one studies (five with control conditions) of relaxation for a variety of pains including temperomandibular joint pain, back pain and arthritis. Some used relaxation combined with biofeedback or additional cognitive strategies. All the studies showed decreases in EMG readings post-treatment, where those measures were used, together with decreases in pain-ratings. In all but two studies, the decreases were significant. At follow-up, pain levels in comparison to discharge were the same or lower except in two studies, in which some patients had maintained progress and some had not. Overall, the results indicate that many pain patients may benefit from relaxation, and Linton suggests that the use of relaxation training as part of a coping skills approach to pain is prudent.

There are difficulties in knowing when some forms of relaxation end and meditation or hypnosis begins, or whether indeed they are essentially the same. Autogenic training, for example, is so-called because it was considered by its originators to be a self-generated form of hypnotic trance; relaxation is induced by self-suggestion. Muscular relaxation induced by a variety of formal and informal methods including Yoga and Transcendental Meditation is characteristically accompanied by changes in brain activity which are similar to those seen in a hypnotic trance (see Delmonte 1984).

Hypnosis

There is ongoing debate about the nature of hypnosis, in particular about whether it is an altered state of consciousness or a sophisticated piece of social interaction between the hypnotist and the patient. Wagstaff (1995) gives a brief account of the debate.

Traditionally, hypnosis is instigated and guided by a therapist (in contrast to autogenic training). There are different forms of hypnotic induction, some of which typically involve instructions designed to promote passivity, reduce sensory and proprioceptive input, narrow the focus of attention, and lower arousal. Budzynski (1971) has suggested that these phenomena are associated with an altered but by no means unique state, akin to drowsiness, in which critical faculties and defences characteristic of a more alert state are weakened, and thus the individual is less in touch with reality and more open to suggestion. The extent to which any of these factors is a necessary part of the proceedings is, however, questionable. Hypnosis used clinically in the treatment of children's pain from traumatic injury (e.g. burns) or associated with procedures such as suturing is often effected by an invitation to collude in a shared story or fantasy, for example. Helmut Karle (personal communication) has described holding out his hands and saying 'I've got two kittens here, a black one and a white one. Which do you want to play with?' as an opening approach. This implies that there is an understanding between the child and the therapist that an imaginative game is to be played. Having accepted the first suggestion, the child is then ready to accept others, which the therapist successively shapes. There is indeed a 'loosening of the reality-oriented frame of reference' and focused attention, but the elements of drowsiness and low arousal are not so obviously present. Karle's observations are in accord with Erickson's view, that hypnosis is a technique of communicating ideas so as to ensure that the patient is maximally receptive. He goes on to talk about the task of securing the patient's attention and leaving him wide open to the acceptance of an idea that fits the situation (Erickson and Rossi 1980, 1981), which leaves aside questions of relaxation or drowsiness, and problems associated with differences in hypnotizability, and concentrates on social interaction. This plethora of different ideas about hypnosis is one of the factors which makes it difficult to evaluate 'it' as a treatment technique.

Various forms of hypnosis have been used in the study and treatment of pain in a number of ways. In laboratory studies, typical techniques involve inducing pain with pressure or ice-water, and giving the suggestion of analgesia. There is much debate about the role of hypnosis versus deception/compliance in these studies, and the matter is as yet unresolved. Clinically, hypnosis has been used in the treatment of many conditions including pain; Bromley (1985) reports on a range of studies claiming efficacy for hypnosis as a treatment for pain in conditions such as temperomandibular joint syndrome, surgery, labour, burns, cancer, headache and phantom limb. Typically, suggestions are given about numbness or sensory transformation or dissociation (removing oneself in fantasy from the painful situation). However, with the range of different techniques described as hypnosis it is usually impossible to determine what it is that is having the therapeutic effect. One study which identified the components of the hypnotic technique used has shed some light on the question. Zelter and LeBaron (1982) compared hypnosis with a 'supportive nonhypnosis distraction intervention' which included deep breathing, in a sample of children and young people aged 6–17 who were undergoing bone marrow aspirations and spinal taps. The hypnotic technique was shown to be more effective than the distraction condition. The technique consisted of imagery and fantasy constructed to suit the individual needs of the children, and its success was ascribed to the imagery component and its power to hold the children's attention. Other studies (see pp. 124–5 on cognitive-behavioural therapy) have also identified imagery as a powerful therapeutic tool in pain management. Bromley (1985) observed that relaxation, distraction and imagery techniques can produce comfort when a patient is not in a trance.

While the origins of hypnosis as a form of treatment for pain go back a long way, biofeedback is as young as the technological revolution which produced the electronic equipment which is a necessary part of the procedure.

Biofeedback

Feedback, or knowledge of results, is the means by which a goal-directed system is adjusted to keep it moving towards its goal. In biofeedback, instruments are used to enhance and transform information from the body, such as the temperature of the skin or the amount of tension in skeletal muscles, into a vivid form like a flashing light or oscilloscope readout, a tone or a series of clicks. In binary feedback there are two states of the feedback signal, and they change from one to the other when a predetermined criterion is reached, for example 25°C skin temperature, signalled by a change in the pitch of a tone or a light coming on. More precise feedback is possible with an analogue signal, where there is a continuous relationship between the signal and the response magnitude, such as a series of clicks which increase in frequency with increased muscle tension, or a needle moving across a dial. Operant conditioning is the learning paradigm in biofeedback; the knowledge of results acts as a reinforcer as it signals success (i.e. a change in the desired direction). In the treatment of pain, physiological parameters subjected to biofeedback conditioning include muscle tone, finger temperature and EEG alpha activity.

Biofeedback as a treatment for physical disorders was pioneered by Neal Miller (1974), who first demonstrated that modification in blood pressure could be achieved with feedback. He argued that operant conditioning was effecting the change; information showing change in the desired direction serves as a reinforcer. Miller's early work was carried out on animals, and demonstrated larger and more consistent changes. He felt that the relatively poorer results achieved in human subjects might be due in part to their capacity to influence visceral activity by voluntary or involuntary changes in skeletal muscle tension or the rate or depth of breathing, and argued that these factors should be controlled in future experiments, as they confounded the demonstration of pure operant conditioning. Be that as it may, biofeedback moved rapidly out of the laboratory into the clinic, and has continued to be used as a therapeutic tool since, although it has rarely demonstrated the efficacy shown in the early animal studies. It may be that

Miller's view of the contaminating effects of changes in breathing and muscle tension is a factor in biofeedback's failure to fulfil its early promise (although it could be argued that these effects could be harnessed to the good), but it is more likely that enthusiasm for the technique has too seldom been matched with enthusiasm for the establishment of adequate baseline measures, appropriate control procedures and careful selection of appropriate techniques for specific problems or specific subsets of patients. Middaugh (1990), for example, re-analysed data from four studies which appeared to show that biofeedback had little specific effect, and showed that within the treatment groups, certain subgroups benefited more than others but that this differential effect was lost in the statistical analysis. Horn (1993) has argued that the efficacy of biofeedback has been hard to evaluate when it has been used to treat conditions in which the link between the physiological process undergoing modification and the disorder undergoing treatment is indirect or not established. For example, several studies have demonstrated positive effects of biofeedback training for pain in the fingers associated with Raynaud's phenomenon, in which peripheral vasoconstriction occurs (Surwit and Fenton 1980; Freedman et al. 1981; Yocum et al. 1985). Temperature feedback was shown to enhance voluntary vasodilation in the fingers in those with the disorder, although some studies showed a differential success rate at follow-up; in some patients elevation of their digital temperature by vasodilation was maintained after treatment and in others it was lost. The reasons for the differences in the maintenance of the conditioned response are not clear, and merit further investigation.

Conditioned digital vasodilation has also been used to treat migraine, a severe form of headache in which the extracranial blood vessels constrict and then dilate, although the link between digital vasodilation and the activity of the extracranial blood vessels is not at all clear. Two arguments have been advanced as rationales for the method:

1 Increased peripheral blood flow is associated with increased muscular relaxation, which might be effective in treating migraine.
2 Increased blood flow to the periphery might cause a corresponding decrease in blood flow to the extracranial vessels, thus reducing vasodilation and so reducing pain.

There are problems with both these arguments. First, muscular relaxation is characteristically accompanied by increased blood flow, but the converse is not true. Second, there is no evidence that increased blood flow to the fingers results in decreased flow in the extracranial vessels. Price and Tursky (1976) and Claghorn et al. (1981) found *increases* in extracranial blood flow and regional cerebral blood flow in association with handwarming, and Dalessio et al. (1979) found *reduced* extracranial flow in migraineurs who were successful in reducing headaches with handwarming. Turk et al. (1979)

have questioned the hypothesis that learned vasomotor control is central to migraine treatment, and have pointed out the failure of studies to demonstrate that reduction in headache incidence is correlated with alteration of peripheral vasodilation or pulse amplitude – a premise on which biofeedback conditioning is based. Later Chapman (1986) carried out a comprehensive review of thermal feedback and EMG studies for migraine and 'tension' headache and found no evidence for a specific contribution of thermal parameters to migraine. Holmes and Burish (1983) also reviewed a number of studies of thermal feedback and migraine, and concluded that there is no firm evidence of its effectiveness as a treatment technique; where an effect appears to have been demonstrated, it is usually related to the relaxation response. Price and Tursky (1976) have also postulated that when a link between handwarming and headache reduction has been shown, it is probably the result of reduced sympathetic arousal.

Another form of biofeedback commonly used in pain control studies is muscle tension feedback from electromyograph (EMG) recordings. It has been used most often to treat so-called tension headache by biofeedback-moderated conditioning of frontalis muscle tension. Some researchers have demonstrated a relationship between increased muscle tension and headache (Budzynski et al. 1973; van Boxtel and van der Ven 1978). Others have failed to find a consistent pattern (Epstein and Abel 1977; Harper and Steger 1978). Tunis and Wolff (1954) found a degree of vasoconstriction in some subjects as well, and Takeshima and Kazuro (1988) suggest that many headache patients show changes in muscle tension and blood flow, and that there is a continuum from classic migraine to typical tension headache. It may be that the assumed direction of causality is wrong in both cases, and that increased muscle tension and changes in blood flow are related phenomena rather than causal.

Although attempts to demonstrate a relationship between EMG and/or thermal parameters and headache parameters have generally failed to produce significant results, studies using pseudofeedback have suggested that in subjects in whom a specific relationship between frontalis muscle tension and pain can be shown, biofeedback conditioning is likely to be effective. Borgeat et al. (1985) demonstrated differential effects of EMG biofeedback on two groups of patients, one group of which demonstrated a positive association between head pain and muscle tension increases, and the other did not. There was no difference between the two groups in terms of clinical improvement with biofeedback, although the shape of the recovery curves varied. The positive association group showed an immediate improvement in headache activity followed by loss of improvement in the second half of treatment, while the no-association group showed a steady sustained improvement in headache activity. There was no relationship between clinical improvement and EMG lowering in either group. Borgeat et al. (1985) postulate the influence of non-specific factors like expectation to explain these results.

Finally, EEG alpha training has been used as a treatment for a variety of conditions, including pain. The rationale for alpha training – that is, the practice of maintaining an alpha rhythm of brain activity – is that it is incompatible with high states of arousal and concentration (Trifiletti 1984) and may therefore interfere with the perception of pain. Trifiletti reports on case studies in which the production of alpha waves occurred simultaneously with activities normally associated with pain, in people who apparently did not feel any pain. Some of these were dramatic demonstrations of analgesia during deep self-inflicted puncture wounds, and the concurrent presence of EEG alpha waves was taken to indicate that there was a causal relationship between them and the analgesia. Some studies have used EEG alpha biofeedback for clinical pain (e.g. Gannon and Sternbach 1971) but the relationship between alpha production and pain is unclear. Alpha waves are normally associated with relaxed, focused attention, and therefore *reflect* a state of mind shown to be conducive to pain control in studies of biofeedback and relaxation. Melzack and Perry (1975) concluded that EEG alpha training was not sufficient to alter subjective pain intensity unless it was combined with procedures such as relaxation and suggestion.

In spite of the inconsistent correspondence between underlying physiological parameters and pain, and the ongoing debate about the aetiology of headache, Chapman (1986) reports on several studies which demonstrate both short-term efficacy and long-term maintenance of success of biofeedback for headache. Several explanations for these successes have been put forward, almost all of them implicating changes in cognitive parameters such as mastery, perceived control, shift towards internality in locus of control, and learned relaxation response. The question then arises as to whether these changes need biofeedback to be effected, or could they be achieved by less expensive and complex means such as relaxation training or cognitive behavioural therapy? Turk *et al.* (1979) have reviewed a number of studies of biofeedback and headache, and have argued that studies show that EMG biofeedback is no more effective for the treatment of tension headache than other approaches such as relaxation or stress coping training, and finger-temperature biofeedback for migraine was no more effective than EEG alpha enhancement or self-hypnosis.

There are good reasons why biofeedback should be helpful in pain control. If the pain is primarily caused by physical factors such as excessive muscle tension or vasoconstriction, then the provision of feedback should, at the very least, aid the conditioning of corrective responses, as Miller (1974) demonstrated.

However, the 'pure' conditioning of physiological responses that Miller hoped for is probably not possible in conscious human subjects; cognitive processes mediate the responses. At a simple level, biofeedback requires a period of focused attention on the machine output, which may act as a distractor. It is also a means of learning self-regulation with specific, clearly signalled goals and goal attainment, so that self-efficacy beliefs may be strengthened. All this being so, it is perhaps surprising that results have not been more impressive, as these factors have been shown to promote pain control. However, when an effect has been shown in biofeedback studies, it has often been impossible to demonstrate that anything other than these 'non-specific' factors were operating, and there are cheaper and less complicated ways of invoking them. Studies have seldom been designed to control for non-specific factors by having them common to all treatment groups. Middaugh (1990) has also demonstrated that treatment effects are lost in the analysis of results of some studies, as there are differential effects with certain parameters (for example, more severe muscle spasm showed greater improvement than moderate spasm) which may not be accounted for. A final possible confound is that some attempts to condition physiological responses have not taken account of the direction of causality, or have concentrated on epiphenomena, and it is therefore not surprising that results from such studies are unconvincing.

Behavioural techniques

Fordyce (1984) pioneered the use of behavioural techniques in the treatment of chronic pain, proposing that

> pain problems are signalled by the behaviour of the patient. Without visible or audible indications from the suffering person that there is a pain problem, in the practical case there is no pain problem . . . pain behaviours, as behaviour, are subject to influence by whatever factors influence behaviour.
>
> (Fordyce 1984: 866)

Fordyce went on to describe pain behaviours as operants, which are sensitive to learning or conditioning effects from contingent reinforcement. The two basic kinds of reinforcement which are contingent on pain behaviour are positive (care or attention is offered when pain behaviour is emitted) and negative (an unpleasant or aversive situation is avoided because of pain behaviour). Studies such as those by Flor *et al.* (1987) and Cairns and Pasino (1977) have shown evidence of operant conditioning in pain behaviour. The extent of conditioning of pain behaviours depends on the expectations of reinforcement from past experience of the sufferer, the extent to which the environment is arranged so as to supply reinforcement, and the persistence of the original nociception: the longer it persists, the more opportunities there are for reinforcement. Chronic pain behaviour has different forms, but common features are the overuse of medication, diminution of activity, resting, dramatization of complaints, and distorted motor behaviour such as limping and guarding. Treatment programmes vary in precise details, but all involve the elimination of the maladaptive pain behaviours by non-reinforcement, and the strengthening of 'well' behaviours by social reinforcers such as praise and attention. Medication is given on a time-contingent rather than pain-contingent basis, and in some programmes is made up into an elixir which is given in the same quantity three times a day while the active ingredient is slowly withdrawn. An initial assessment determines medication need and exercise/activity tolerance, and exercise quotas are set so that they begin at or below baseline and increase slowly day by day. (Doleys *et al.* (1982) among others have demonstrated the positive effect of exercise quotas on pain behaviour.) Rest is contingent upon achieving quota. Patients are helped to develop alternative behaviours; as Fordyce (1984) has said, it is easier to increase standing and walking times than to decrease resting time, although there is obviously a reciprocal relationship. Alternative behaviours might include relaxation techniques, hobbies, walking and other forms of gentle exercise (to recover lost muscle tone and replace sitting or resting for long periods). The programme is typically six weeks of inpatient treatment and is set up in consultation with the patient and the family.

Some critics have argued that the behavioural treatment programme moderates only the outward signs of pain but does nothing for the underlying pain experience. If this were true, it would have achieved precisely what Fordyce claimed for it; his view is that the technique is designed to combat the disability associated with the pain. It is common, however, for patients to report a decrease in pain levels and a heightened sense of well-being as the programme progresses and activity levels increase. There are many possible explanations for the decrease in reported pain levels. On a simple level, pre-programme activity levels are characteristically low, and much time is spent resting, so that there are many opportunities for pain to be the focus of attention. During the programme, the days are full and there are many opportunities for distraction from the pain. Exercise helps to rebuild muscle and to counteract the physical effects of disuse, which may in themselves be pain-producing. Coping skills and mastery are developed, which may have an impact on self-referent beliefs associated with pain.

Linton (1982) among others has written a critical review of behavioural pain management programmes, and has commented on the low number of studies with a control condition, and the high numbers of rejections, refusals and dropouts in the studies. However, in the fifteen studies Linton considered, increases in activity levels were reported in every one. Large reductions in medication intake were typically reported. Subjective pain ratings were generally lowered, but only by a moderate amount. These gains were maintained at follow-up.

It may be argued that there is no such thing as a purely behavioural approach to pain in humans, just as it has been argued here that 'pure' biofeedback conditioning of physiological states is not possible in a conscious human subject. Cognitions are bound to be having an effect. The difference between behavioural and cognitive-behavioural approaches, however, is that in the latter cognitive parameters are believed to be central factors in behaviour and as such are the focus of treatment and worked with in a planned and structured way.

Cognitive-behaviour therapy

The power of cognitive factors in moderating pain has already been discussed (see pp. 71–9). At the most basic level, distraction (or attention focused elsewhere) has been shown to be effective in reducing the pain associated with acute trauma or aversive medical procedures. Expectations and beliefs, whether they are about the pain or one's capacity to cope with it, have also been shown to exert considerable influence on pain. Cognitive-behaviour therapy (CBT) as described by Turk and Fernandez (1991) begins with two assumptions. First, cognition, affect, motivation and behaviour are reciprocally causally related. Second, people are constantly engaged in adaptive behaviour – appraising the meaning of novel stimuli and making judgements about their capacity to deal with it. Threat – that is an event perceived as disruptive or potentially disruptive, such as illness or pain – invokes physiological, psychological and behavioural responses, and an effective therapeutic method needs to take account of all of them. CBT focuses on appraisal, interpretation and expectancies as well as physiological and environmental influences (Turk and Rudy 1989). Turk and Fernandez (1991) identify three foci of CBT interventions for cancer pain:

◆ alteration of maladaptive behaviours
◆ alteration of ongoing self-statements, images and feelings that interfere with adaptive functioning
◆ alteration of tacit assumptions and beliefs that give rise to habitual maladaptive ways of construing the self (e.g. as helpless) and the cancer (or the pain) as uncontrollable.

The intervention begins with assessment and information exchange, so that there is a baseline and a detailed account of the problem for the therapist, and accurate facts to facilitate adaptation by the patient. In chronic pain patients, for example, information about the gating mechanism and how it operates might be given to dispel fears about perceived malignancy and correct the notion that the involvement of a psychologist suggests that the pain has been appraised as imaginary by the doctor. In surgery or procedural pain, information about precisely what will happen and how long it will last may be given in order to prevent inaccurate expectations leading to raised anxiety.

CBT programmes are collaborative endeavours between the patient and the therapist; after the initial assessment they agree on the programme of intervention so that a sense of personal control and self-efficacy is facilitated. There are several elements in the CBT programme; reconceptualization of the problem and cognitive restructuring, skills teaching (problem-solving, relaxation, imagery, attention-diversion) and consolidation of the skills through practice. Generalization and maintenance of skills are also addressed, and follow-up.

CBT has been shown to be effective with children in acute pain. It has been used to help children cope with painful medical treatments after burn injury (Elliott and Olson 1983), and during bone marrow aspirations and spinal taps (Jay et al. 1985). Jay and colleagues developed the CBT package, consisting of filmed modelling, positive reinforcement, breathing exercises, imagery/distraction and behavioural rehearsal.

A rich and multidimensional package of treatment such as the one outlined by Turk and Fernandez (1991) makes assessment of efficacy difficult. Which are the crucial elements? If results are less than optimal, how will the cause be established from among so many variables? Syrjala et al. (1995) compared four groups of cancer patients undergoing painful treatment, in a controlled study. The groups were: treatment as usual, therapist support, relaxation and imagery training, and a package of cognitive-behavioural skills which included relaxation and imagery training. Results showed that patients who received the package and the relaxation plus imagery reported less pain than the other two groups, but there was no evidence that the CBT package conferred any additional benefit over and above the relaxation plus imagery. In a study of patients with low back pain, Turner and Jensen (1993) found that all three treatment groups – relaxation with imagery, CBT, and CBT with relaxation and imagery, reported reductions in pain compared to a no-treatment group. Syrjala et al. (1995) comment on the findings of these and other studies, all of which appear to show that imagery is the salient factor in pain control.

Studies have tended to show that CBT is effective in a range of painful conditions, but the whole package is not more effective than some of its component parts, such as relaxation and imagery. It may be that coping and other skills explicitly addressed in CBT are implicitly conditioned as successful relaxation or imagery is attained and experienced as effective.

Conclusion

A range of psychological techniques has been developed and used in laboratory and clinical studies of pain control. Those described in this chapter are a sample of the most widely used models. All of them attempt, implicitly or explicitly, to change the way that pain is conceptualized, and to modify maladaptive behaviours, be they overt as in excessive resting, or covert as in catastrophic thinking. They have not always been adequately assessed in research studies, which has made it difficult to discover which factors are operating to effect change. The issue of non-specific factors is an interesting one. Non-specific factors include not only the placebo effect, which is common to all forms of therapeutic intervention, but also factors such as relaxation and focused attention if they have not been assessed or controlled for. The effectiveness of an intervention cannot be known unless its effect on covert as well as overt behaviour is assessed, and this has too often been neglected. As a result, there exists a number of psychological interventions which seem to be effective, to a greater or lesser degree, in clinical populations, but which cannot always be shown to perform well in research studies. It may be that research methods with sufficient rigour and imaginativeness to capture the essence of the processes of change have yet to be developed.

References

Benson, H. (1975) *The Relaxation Response*. New York: William Morrow.

Borgeat, F., Elie, R. and Larouche, L.M. (1985) Pain response to voluntary muscle tension increases and biofeedback efficacy in tension headaches. *Headache*, 25: 387–91.

Bromley, S.P. (1985) Treatment of pain: theory and research, in R.P. Zahourek (ed.) *Clinical Hypnosis and Therapeutic Suggestion in Nursing*. Orlando, FL: Grune and Stratton.

Budzynski, T.H. (1971) Some applications of biofeedback-produced twilight states. Paper presented at the American Psychological Association Convention, Washington, DC.

Budzynski, T.H., Stoyva, J., Adler, C.S. and Mullaney, D.J. (1973) EMG biofeedback and tension headache: a controlled outcome study. *Psychosomatic Medicine*, 35: 484–96.

Cairns, D. and Pasino, J. (1977) Comparison of verbal reinforcement and feedback in the operant treatment of disability of chronic low back pain. *Behaviour Therapy*, 8: 621–30.

Chapman, S.L. (1986) A review and clinical perspective on the use of EMG and thermal feedback for chronic headaches. *Pain*, 27: 1–43.

Claghorn, J.L., Mathew, R.J., Largen, J.W. and Meyer, J.S. (1981) Directional effects of skin temperature regulation on regional cerebral blood flow in normal subjects and migraine patients. *American Journal of Psychiatry*, 138: 1182–7.

Dalessio, D.J., Kunzel, M., Sternbach, R. and Sovak, M. (1979) Conditioned adaptation-relaxation reflex in migraine therapy. *Journal of the American Medical Association*, 242: 2102–4.

Delmonte, M.M. (1984) Meditation: similarities with hypnoidal states and hypnosis. *International Journal of Psychosomatics*, 31: 24–34.

Doleys, D.M., Crocker, M. and Patton, D. (1982) Response of patients with chronic pain to exercise quotas. *Physical Therapy*, 62: 1111–15.

Elliott, C.H. and Olson, R.A. (1983) The management of children's distress in response to painful medical treatment for burn injuries. *Behaviour Research and Therapy*, 21: 675–83.

Epstein, L.H. and Abel, G.G. (1977) An analysis of training effects for tension headache patients. *Behaviour Therapy*, 8: 37–47.

Erickson, M. and Rossi, E. (1980) *Innovative Hypnotherapy: The Collected Papers of Milton H. Erickson on Hypnosis vol. IV.* New York: Irvington.

Erickson, M. and Rossi, E. (1981) *Experiencing Hypnosis.* New York: Irvington.

Flor, H., Kerns, R.D. and Turk, D.C. (1987) The role of the spouse in the maintenance of chronic pain. *Journal of Psychosomatic Research*, 31: 251–60.

Fordyce, W.E. (1984) Behavioural science and chronic pain. *Postgraduate Medical Journal*, 60: 865–8.

Freedman, R.R., Lynn, S.J., Ianni, P. and Hale, P.A. (1981) Biofeedback treatment of Raynaud's disease and phenomenon. *Biofeedback and Self-regulation*, 6: 355–65.

Gannon, L. and Sternbach, R.A. (1971) Alpha enhancement as a treatment for pain: a case study. *Journal of Behaviour Therapy and Experimental Psychiatry*, 2: 209.

Harper, R.G. and Steger, J.C. (1978) Psychological correlates of frontalis EMG and pain in tension headache. *Headache*, 18: 215–18.

Holmes, D.S. and Burish, T.G. (1983) Effectiveness of biofeedback for treating migraine and tension headache: a review of the evidence. *Journal of Psychosomatic Research*, 27: 515–32.

Horn, S. (1993) Biofeedback, in G.T. Lewith and D. Aldridge (eds) *Clinical Research Methodology for Complementary Therapies.* London: Hodder and Stoughton.

Jacobson, E. (1938) *Progressive Relaxation.* Urbana, IL: University of Chicago Press.

Jay, S.M., Elliott, C.M., Ozolins, M., Olson, R. and Pruitt, S. (1985) Behavioural management of children's distress during painful medical procedures. *Behaviour Research and Therapy*, 23: 513–20.

Lehrer, P.M. (1982) How to relax and how not to relax: a re-evaluation of the work of Edmund Jacobson. *Journal of Behaviour Research and Therapy*, 20: 417–28.

Linton, S. (1982) A critical review of behavioural treatments for chronic benign pain other than headache. *British Journal of Clinical Psychology*, 21: 321–37.

Luthe, W. and Schultz, J.H. (1969) *Autogenic Therapy.* New York: Grune and Stratton.

McCauley, J.D., Frank, R.G. and Callen, K.E. (1983) Hypnosis compared to relaxation in the outpatient management of chronic low back pain. *Archives of Physical Medicine and Rehabilitation*, 64: 548–52.

Melzack, R. and Perry, C. (1975) Self-regulation of pain: the use of alpha-feedback and hypnotic training for the control of chronic pain. *Experimental Neurology*, 46: 452–69.

Melzack, R. and Wall, P.D. (1982) *The Challenge of Pain.* Harmondsworth: Penguin.

Middaugh, S.J. (1990) On clinical efficacy: why biofeedback does – and does not – work. *Biofeedback and Self-regulation*, 15: 191–208.

Miller, N.E. (1974) Biofeedback: evaluation of a new technic. *New England Journal of Medicine*, 290: 684–5.

Price, K.P. and Tursky, B. (1976) Vascular reactivity of migraineurs and nonmigraineurs: a comparison of responses to self-control procedures. *Headache*, 16: 210–17.

Solbach, P., Sargent, J. and Coyne, L. (1984) Menstrual migraine headache: results of a controlled, experimental, outcome study of nondrug treatments. *Headache*, 24: 75–8.

Sternbach, R.A. (1984) Recent advances in psychologic pain therapy. *Advances in Pain Research and Therapy*, 7: 251–5.

Stewart, M.L. (1977) Measurement of clinical pain, in A.K. Jacox (ed.) *Pain: A Source Book for Nurses and Other Health Professionals.* Boston, MA: Little, Brown.

Surwit, R.S. and Fenton, C.H. (1980) Feedback and instructions in the control of digital temperature. *Psychophysiology*, 17: 129–32.

Syrjala, K.L., Donaldson, G.W., Davis, M.W., Kippes, M.E. and Carr, J.E. (1995) Relaxation and imagery or cognitive–behavioural training reduce pain during cancer treatment: a controlled clinical trial. *Pain*, 62: 189–98.

Takeshima, T. and Kazuro, K. (1988) The relationship between muscle contraction headache and migraine: a multivariate analysis. *Headache*, 28: 272–7.

Tesler, M., Ward, J. and Savedra, M. (1983) Developing an instrument for eliciting children's description of pain. *Perceptual and Motor Skills*, 56: 315–21.

Thompson, K.L. and Varni, J.W. (1986) A developmental cognitive–behavioural approach to paediatric pain assessment. *Pain*, 25: 283–96.

Trifiletti, R.J. (1984) The psychological effectiveness of pain management procedures in the context of behavioural medicine and medical psychology. *Genetic Psychology Monographs*, 109: 251–78.

Tunis, M.M. and Wolff, H.G. (1954) Studies on headache: cranial artery vasoconstriction and muscle contraction headache. *Archives of Neurology and Psychiatry*, 71: 425–34.

Turk, D.C. and Fernandez, E. (1991) Pain: A cognitive–behavioural perspective, in M. Watson (ed.) *Cancer Patient Care: Psychosocial Treatment Methods*. Cambridge: BPS Books.

Turk, D.C. and Rudy, T.E. (1989) An integrated approach to pain treatment: beyond the scalpel and the syringe, in C.D. Tollison (ed.) *Handbook of Chronic Pain Management*. Baltimore, MD: Williams and Wilkins.

Turk, D.C., Meichenbaum, D.H. and Berman, W.H. (1979) Application of biofeedback for the regulation of pain: a critical review. *Psychological Bulletin*, 86: 1322–38.

Turk, D.C., Meichenbaum, D. and Genest, M. (1983) *Pain and Behavioural Medicine: A Cognitive-Behavioural Perspective*. New York: Guilford Press.

Turner, J.A. and Jensen, M.P. (1993) Efficacy of cognitive therapy for chronic low back pain. *Pain*, 52: 169–77.

van Boxtel, A. and van der Ven, J.R. (1978) Differential EMG activity in subjects with muscle contraction headache related to mental effort. *Headache*, 17: 233–7.

Varni, J.W., Thompson, K.L. and Hanson, V. (1987) The Varni/Thompson Pediatric Pain Questionnaire. 1. Chronic musculoskeletal pain in juvenile rheumatoid arthritis. *Pain*, 28: 27–38.

Wagstaff, G. (1995) Hypnosis, in A.M. Colman (ed.) *Controversies in Psychology*. New York: Longman.

Wall, P.D. (1979) On the relation of injury to pain. The John J. Bonica Lecture. *Pain*, 6: 253–64.

Yocum, D.E., Hodes, R., Sundstrom, W.R. and Cleeland, S. (1985) Use of biofeedback training in treatment of Raynaud's disease and phenomenon. *Journal of Rheumatology*, 12: 90–3.

Zelter, L.K. and LeBaron, S. (1982) Hypnosis and nonhypnotic techniques for reduction of pain and anxiety during painful procedures in children and adolescents with cancer. *Journal of Paediatrics*, 101: 1032–5.

 Conclusion

The intention herein has been to highlight the problems faced by both the theoretician and the clinician tackling the question of human pain. While solutions are alluded to, and effective interventions for treatment and management described, there is still a tendency for much of the literature to be descriptive and fragmented. The different conceptions of what constitutes pain, assumed at the outset of varied research projects, result in findings that are not necessarily directly comparable. One theme of this book, then, has been to suggest ways in which these different conceptions and models can be brought together: gate control theory provided the basis for this, highlighting the very real role of factors previously dismissed by the majority of pain researchers, and providing a theoretical framework for this. While gate control theory is certainly not beyond criticism, it illustrates the conceptual shift sometimes required if a field of research is to progress.

One major source of confusion has stemmed from the psychophysical history of research into pain sensation, and the linguistic confusion surrounding our use of the word 'pain'. While psychophysicists can boast a wealth of successes in analysing the details of perceptual processes such as vision and hearing, this success has not translated equally to pain, although there have been valuable findings. The point here is that in the case of pain, language suggests that there should be an object which the pain refers to, an internal mental entity. Pain, however, is not a perceptual process: while we say that we perceive a physical object or a sound, we do not (in normal language) say the same about pain. Instead we *feel* pain, and the importance of this distinction has perhaps been underestimated: the cause of the pain may be an object, but the pain itself is not. It is related to Wall's observation that pain is best typified as a need state; we feel hunger, which is a need state, and the same grammar appears to apply to pain. In other words, the source of much confusion has been the attempt to force the logic of pain grammar into that of perceptual grammar. This is not to say that, as a sensory process, pain can be adequately described by the action of sensory nerve fibres alone: hunger can be modulated by distraction, for example, and so can pain. Instead what is required is an acceptance that a sensory process, subsumed primarily by a physiological system, can in fact be far more complex and subtle, and far wider ranging in scope, than has previously been acknowledged.

To an extent this debate is of limited importance to those concerned with the adequate treatment and management of pain and painful conditions. Here the description of a treatment programme with measurably superior effects to others would be sufficient support for the adoption of that programme. This, however, denies the importance of allying practice to theory, in that the development of testable hypotheses can in itself suggest ways in which existing treatments can be developed and improved. That is, a more complete understanding of the issues, conceptual, methodological and practical, can only be of benefit: the theoretician borrows phenomena described by clinicians that must be explained by a complete model, while the clinician borrows models from the theoretician that describe potential methods of treatment. This point may seem obvious, but it is perhaps surprising the lack of cross-disciplinary understanding that is apparent from an even cursory review of the literature.

Glossary of neurophysiological and anatomical terms

A-beta fibre (cutaneous) Myelinated nerve fibres which respond to mechanical stimuli such as light pressure and vibration.

A-delta fibre (cutaneous) Myelinated nerve fibres which may be stimulated by pressure, heat, cooling or locally produced chemicals. Classically, activation was believed to generate such sensations as temperature and fast pricking pain ('first pain'); this view is now recognized as simplistic (for a recent discussion, see Melzack and Wall 1996: 86 *et seq.*).

Acupuncture Therapeutic technique for treating certain painful (and other) conditions by stimulating specific areas on the body surface, classically by inserting long thin needles through the skin and stimulating cutaneous nerve fibres.

Afferent Nerve impulses flowing into the central nervous system; consciously perceived afferent information is described as sensory.

B-endorphin One of the endogenous opioids.

C-fibre Unmyelinated nerve fibres which can respond to similar stimuli to A-delta fibres. Classically, they were considered to transmit dull, persistent or burning pain ('second pain').

Catecholamines Biologically active amines (organic molecules containing nitrogen in amino groups); they have a marked effect on the nervous and cardiovascular systems, metabolic rate, body temperature and smooth muscle activity. Includes the sympathetic transmitters noradrenaline and adrenaline (epinephrine in American usage) as well as the important central neurotransmitter dopamine.

Causalgia Intense burning pain triggered by normally innocuous stimuli; often a long term consequence of peripheral nerve damage, particularly from tearing injuries.

Central neural plasticity The ability of the CNS to be moulded by exogenous and endogenous stimuli, so that its function is modified. Changes may be permanent or semi-permanent.

CNS Central nervous system.

Deafferentation Abolition of the afferent nerve inputs to a region of the CNS; excision, transection or blocking of the sensory nerve supply by surgery, trauma or disease.

Dorsal horns The region of the spinal cord adjacent to the dorsal spinal nerve roots through which afferent information enters. Usually referred to as posterior horns in human anatomy due to the vertical orientation of the human spinal column.

Endogenous opioids Chemical substances (polypeptides) produced in the brain that produce analgesia by binding to opiate receptor sites involved in pain perception.

Hyperalgesia Excessive sensitivity to pain.

Internal capsule A bundle of myelinated nerve fibres in the forebrain, carrying inputs and outputs from the cerebral cortex and other structures.

Ischaemia Local deficiency of blood supply due to obstruction of the circulation.

Medulla In this context, the hindmost region of the brain; the portion adjacent to the spinal cord.

Myelinated fibre Nerve fibre wrapped in layers of protein-containing lipid ('fatty') cell membranes formed by satellite cells. This greatly increases the speed of action potential conduction.

Naloxone A drug that binds to opioid receptors and prevents or reverses the action of morphine and other opioid drugs. Used clinically to treat narcotic overdose.

Neuroma (plural neuromata) In this context, refers to a tangle of nerve fibre tips formed after a peripheral nerve is cut or damaged.

Neurotransmitter Substance released when the axon terminal of a presynaptic neuron is excited, which then diffuses across the synaptic gap to act on the target cell.

Nociception Afferent input signalling imminent or actual tissue damage.

Palmar sweat index Measurement of sweat gland activity on the palm of the hand, used as a measure of sympathetic nervous activity and stress.

Peptide A class of biologically active molecules consisting of amino acids joined together in chains. When the number of amino acids is large, they are usually referred to as proteins.

Phantom limb Following amputation of a limb, the patient frequently feels as if the limb still exists. The sensation of pain coming from the amputated part of the limb is known as *phantom limb pain*.

Receptive field The area within which appropriate stimulation will cause action potentials in a single nerve fibre.

Sensory-motor cortex In animals, an area of the cerebral cortex in which sensory information is received and motor signals are generated. In the human brain the functions tend to be carried out by discrete anatomical areas.

Shock-induced analgesia This is produced by shock, usually electrical, to the organism (also stress induced analgesia).

Signal-detection theory (STD) A body of concepts related to the perception of signals against a background of noise.

Somesthetic Used to describe sensations arising from stimulation of sensory receptors on the surface of the body.

Spinothalamic tract One of the ascending pathways for sensory impulses that travel through the spinal cord to the thalamus.

Substance P A peptide believed to be the primary afferent neurotransmitter of pain information.

Substantia gelatinosa A region of spinal cord grey matter, found in the dorsal horns and adjacent to the central canal.

Summation, spatial and temporal Cumulative effect of stimuli, either over an area or over time.

T-cells In this context, refers to cells in the dorsal horn of the spinal cord which control transmission of nociceptive information to the brain.

Bibliography

Carlson, J.G. and Seifert, A.R. (eds) (1991) *International Perspectives on Self-regulation and Health*. New York: Plenum Press.

Gibson, H.B. (ed.) (1994) *Psychology, Pain and Anaesthesia*. London: Chapman and Hall.

Hilgard, E.R. and Hilgard, J.R. (1983) *Hypnosis in the Relief of Pain*. Los Altos, CA: William Kaufmann, Inc.

Jacox, A.K. (1977) *Pain: A Source Book for Nurses and Other Health Professionals*. Boston, MA: Little, Brown.

Melzack, R. & Wall, P.D. (1982) *The Challenge of Pain*. Harmondsworth: Penguin.

Melzack, R. & Wall, P.D. (1996) *The Challenge of Pain* (rev. 2nd edn). Harmondsworth: Penguin.

Payne, J.P. & Burt, R.A.P. (1972) *Pain: Basic Principles, Pharmacology, Therapy*. Edinburgh and New York: Churchill Livingstone.

Skevington, S.M. (1995) *Psychology of Pain*. Chichester: John Wiley and Sons.

Turk, D.C. & Melzack, R. (ed.) (1992) *Handbook of Pain Assessment*. New York: Guilford Press.

Wall, P.D. & Melzack, R. (eds) (1984) *Textbook of Pain*. Edinburgh and New York: Churchill Livingstone.

Wall, P.D. and Melzack, R. (eds) (1994) *Textbook of Pain* (rev. 3rd edn). Edinburgh and New York: Churchill Livingstone.

Wu, W.-H. (ed.) (1987) *Pain Management*. New York: Human Sciences Press.

Index